NEW
CREATION

NEW
CREATION

**The story of a disciple, his dad, and the dream
of starting a church in washington, dc**

ZACK RANDLES

XULON PRESS

Xulon Press
2301 Lucien Way #415
Maitland, FL 32751
407.339.4217
www.xulonpress.com

Printed in the United States of America.

ISBN-13: 978-1-54566-133-8

Dedication

That we might remember the miracle

Dear Reader,

Books are often written and read for either information or entertainment. It is rare when a book is both instructional and entertaining—and even rarer when that book is a love story.

As you read the history of Waterfront Church DC, you will soon realize there are parallel love stories—that of Jesus Christ for His people, His church, and that of a father and son.

Zack Randles, the founding pastor of Waterfront, ably describes these parallel journeys; and there is wisdom at every turn. You may be thinking you will never "plant" or begin a new church, but the principles of living a Christ-filled life on a daily basis are very much the same. You will discover Biblical truths in every chapter of this journey that you can incorporate into your own life. From your willingness to lead a Christ-centered life to following God's leadership, and stepping out in obedience, your faith and relationship with Jesus will grow ever stronger as you watch God be faithful.

My wife, Dana, and I were fortunate to personally participate in and observe portions of Zack's journey as he laid the cornerstones of Waterfront. I am sure this love story will bless you as it has blessed us.

Most sincerely,
Randy Neugebauer
Texas 19th Congressional District, 2003-2017

Raised in a Baptist church, where I accepted Christ as my Savior 51 years ago, I recognized this young church as the real thing. As Pastor Zack details in this book, the Lord has guided the Randles' efforts with Waterfront Church as it now hosts a vibrant musical program, a group of elders, and a network of supporters who have invested in the church, including Zack's late father, whose guidance in this process has been evident throughout. People are excited about Waterfront, and their dedication in the ongoing miracle is contagious. In a capsule: Congregants come for company and community and continue coming for communion with Christ.

–Eric Whitaker,
United States Ambassador to Niger

Zack and Autumn Randles have modeled faith and courage for many of us. Zack left a secure position with a fixed salary to move to Washington, D.C. to implement the vision that God had given him. Just as God rewarded Abraham for obedience, God has rewarded Zack and Autumn for theirs. Over and over again, God has provided for Waterfront Church DC at just the right time in just the right way.

–David Godfrey,
Attorney & Waterfront Church's first board member

To say this story is anything less than a miracle is truly to sell it short. The way that God has intricately woven all of these events and personalities together to place a church on The Hill is beyond amazing. Zack and Autumn's obedience and personal sacrifice has paid huge dividends in the lives of those affected by this ministry called Waterfront Church D.C. May the Lord continue to bless and protect the work He started years ago in the heart of a college kid in Oklahoma. Go Strong!

–Scott Hicks,
Farmer, Entrepreneur and Waterfront Church
Board Member

It's always inspiring to see someone not just talk about vision but to watch them actually take the steps necessary to see that vision become reality. It has been so cool watching and supporting Zack follow God's leading on every level. This story of Zack Randles, his family, faith, and church planting endeavor will both challenge and inspire you to follow Jesus in a powerful way.

–Dr. Brad Jurkovich,
Senior Pastor, First Bossier Church, Bossier City, LA

This book is a treasure! It is also an inspiration for anyone searching, convicting for those pursuing, and a confirmation for anyone serving! God's majesty and perfection are wonderfully illustrated through this story of the calling and obedience of Zack and Autumn Randles to establish and launch WFC DC. We are so blessed to be part of the "Growth" chapter of WFC DC's history arriving two years after its start. We had moved to D.C. for a specific chapter of service in our own lives, with the mindset of Isaiah's prayer: "Here I am Lord, send me." He sent us to WFC DC! Of all the churches in the D.C. area, the one that was right for us was in our own backyard. We knew WFC DC was our church home the moment we met Zack and saw his passion for sharing Christ and his heart for missions.

–Luke and Leanna McCollum,
United States Navy

Table of Contents

Foreword

Have you ever walked by a church building and wondered about the story behind how it came to be? Who was that original person to whom God gave the vision for starting the church? Why did he choose that location? Who came alongside to help him? How did they find the resources to do it? What struggles did they face in their personal lives? Did the original pastor stay true to the vision and calling God gave or did other things creep in, create disaster for his ministry and wreak havoc on his life and the church?

I have the joy of serving in a role in which I get to see the very beginnings of hundreds of churches every year. As you might expect, there are many challenges, struggles and heartaches along with the victories.

Each year, we partner with hundreds of church planting missionaries as they begin their journey toward starting a church. They head off to difficult places. Some are not wanted where they are going. They have to find new friends, new doctors and new schools for their children. For many, it's a move from the security of a place where they made a nice living, had a nice home and lived in a safe neighborhood. Now they face big expenses, inconveniences, crime and other challenges.

I am blessed to meet and interact with many of these men. Each week, I phone several of them to see how they are doing and ask how we can help and pray for them.

But, so much happens in the life of a church planter even before the part I get to witness. And so much more happens after the role I play is concluded. It reminds me that if we are faithful, God wants to use each one of us in this process of starting and sustaining new churches. We all have a part.

So often we won't see the complete picture this side of heaven. How lives were touched and changed by something we said or an offering we gave or a prayer we prayed. But Zack's story, shared here, gives us that unique opportunity. As you read his remembrances, I hope it reminds you that for every missionary who serves, there are similar stories. Even before they respond to God's call to the mission field there are spiritual battles, family crises, health concerns and financial struggles to deal with

Ministry of this kind is a huge faith stretch and almost without exception, it brings the missionary to a faith crisis in his life. For some, that crisis must occur before they can even surrender to God's call. For others, it happens after they have said "yes," when the reality of their "yes" really begins to set in. For others, it is much later.

Each of these stories are individual, but each is woven into a dozen other stories that all come together to birth the beginnings of a church that then touches hundreds of other lives.

Watching God work through Zack and his family has been one of the most incredible encouragements to me in my role as leader of the North American Mission Board. If you are not familiar with his story, you will quickly see as you read that God Himself has established Waterfront Church. He wanted it there in a strategic location in our nation's capital, and for this, He brought the people and the circumstances and the resources together. That is the only explanation for what has happened.

Zack's story is especially sweet to me because I also had the pleasure of knowing his dear father, Jon. Like many father-son relationships, theirs had a few years of struggle. But, never was there a father who was prouder of how his son responded to God's call and walked faithfully with Him. To see Jon's spiritual legacy in Zack's ministry is such a blessing.

I hope the next time you walk by a church building it will remind you to pray for that church and the one who pastors it. I also hope you will pray for Zack and everyone who is touched by his ministry at Waterfront. His story will help you more effectively pray for the thousands of missionaries, just like him, who are starting churches throughout North America and the world. May their faith be emboldened, and their numbers multiplied.

Kevin Ezell
President
North American Mission Board, SBC
Alpharetta, GA

Introduction

As a child, I was obsessed with roller coasters. The twists, turns, drops, and screams are captivating to a young mind, even if you lack the courage to ride. My first roller coaster memory happened when I was about 5 years old in Graham, Texas. A carnival came in and set up in our downtown. Their crew had blocked the street in front of our friend's home, and my Dad and I watched from their entry steps as they built the haunted house, the hall of mirrors and that amazing roller coaster. This particular coaster was called the "super loop." It was not very complex, literally just a circular track taking riders around and around. I was too young and too short to ride, but I couldn't take my eyes off of it. My mom, realizing my budding obsession, attempted to redirect my attention.

She offered to take me to an amusement park that had some rides more my speed and age appropriate. I was so excited! My Dad even attached scripture memory to the proposal, and some of the first verses I ever memorized were to earn the ticket to that amusement park to experience the roller coasters. So many things in life can be less than expected, but my first day at an amusement park was not one of them. It was glorious, and I didn't even care that most of the rides would have to wait for a future taller me to ride. The lines were also long, but it didn't even matter because of my building anticipation. Year after year I went back to the amusement park, and year after year, I would ride more rides. I would even research amusement parks to figure out what rides they had, and which rides I had not yet ridden.

One day, I was having lunch with a beautiful woman that would eventually be my wife. Her name is Autumn, and you'll be hearing more about her later in the story. We had only been dating a few weeks and the subject of roller coasters made its way into our conversation. She was also a roller coaster junkie, and we immediately began sharing stories of coasters conquered and parks visited. One of the stories she told was particularly memorable. Most roller coaster discussions inevitably lead to a dark question; have you ever gotten sick on one? This is a question with some depth to it. Sometimes, wooden roller coasters can jerk the rider around a bit so they can cause you to feel sick. Sometimes, fast roller coasters can make you blackout so they can cause you to feel sick. Sometimes roller coasters spin or go upside down and that can cause you to feel sick. However, nothing can make even the most experienced rider sick with consistency like mere repetition. Man was not meant to ride a roller coaster constantly without a break in the action.

Autumn began to tell a story about one afternoon at Six Flags Over Texas when she and a friend were waiting in line to ride Titan, which at the time, was the newest, fastest and biggest ride at the park. Titan is a metal roller coaster with smooth turns, steep drops and a consistently long line. This particular day, there had been lots of afternoon rain and the park had cleared out its typical mass of people. Autumn and her friend were shocked to find no one getting in line behind them for the ride. As they climbed in their seats, anticipation was building, and the ride did not disappoint.

She had ridden it before and the experience was all that she had remembered, but as the coaster car pulled back into the starting position, there was no one waiting in line to go next. Autumn looked for the operator and asked kindly, "If no one is in line, can we go again?" What a bold move! The coaster car operator, seeing nothing wrong with this proposal, said, "Sure, you can ride as many times as you want until someone steps in line for your row." She got me hooked on the story. I had to know – "How many times in a row did you ride?" She smiled and said the number 9. Whoa! "It was fun in the beginning," she added. "Ride two and three were exhilarating, but by the time we got to the 9th, we were wishing we had gotten off the ride sooner. It was definitely not meant to be ridden that many times in a row."

As I've gotten older, my body won't allow me to ride as many roller coasters as I once was able to, but I still love to ride, and a strategically placed experience on one here and there makes for great memories with my kiddos.

A person's life is a lot like a roller coaster. There are ups, down, twists, turns, rushes, screams, moments of terror, and moments of triumph, just to name a few. Everyone's life is their own roller coaster and having someone else ride with us over and over again without a break is not exactly healthy or realistic. However, a strategically placed ride here and there can provide fresh perspective, new ideas and hopefully empower the Holy Spirit to stir your heart in a new and exciting way. I'd like to ask you to take a journey with me, to 'ride a round on the roller coaster,' as we look back at the new creation our God has been sculpting that would become Waterfront Church in Washington, DC. The church is a true miracle that is based less than a mile south of the Capitol building, and it began from nothing more than a God-given idea.

Only twice in my life have I ever heard what I believe to be the audible voice of God. When I was younger I always hoped for a moment when that would happen, and I consistently wondered why God did not speak audibly more often to his followers. Through our story, I now have a greater understanding of why. God's desire in any story you are living out is that you would exhibit and exercise faith. The writer of Hebrews even goes so far to say that, "without faith, it is impossible to please God." I strongly believe that the volume of God's voice is directly connected to our exhibition of faith, but not like you would think. If God can increase your faith output by remaining audibly silent as you depend on his scriptures and the conviction Holy Spirit for direction, I believe he will utilize that plan. However, if he can increase your faith output by turning up the volume and presenting you with a completely impossible, on your own, no clue how it will turn out, journey of spiritually clawing for every inch forward toward His divine plan. That being said, this roller coaster of a story both begins and ends with moments in which I believe I heard the audible voice of God. I suppose whether or not you believe me and keep reading from this point is a matter of faith in your own heart as well. I can only tell you my story and then you must decide for yourself. But, let me warn you; this story is saturated in the supernatural. Those of you reading this that know me well know that I am not the smartest guy in the room or even the most capable to plant a church, let alone a church placed in our nation's capital with so many brilliant and ambitious people. Therein lies the reason I believe God chose me for this work and sent His miraculous vision to detail it— because it would require gobs and gobs of faith. If God could be likened to a great artist, His plans begins as a blank canvas that He eventually covers from end to end in faith. The end product is a masterpiece for eternity.

We forget sometimes because God has so many unparalleled attributes, that he is the great creator. God is the grand designer of all things large and small. His artistic sense is unmatched, and he is hard at work in and through our lives creating new things. One of the verses I memorized to get the amusement park ticket when I was 5 years old was 2 Corinthians 5:17. It says, "therefore, if anyone is in Christ they are a new creation, the old has gone, and behold the new has come." Our look into God's craftsmanship will run through the grid of this verse. Through the shed blood of Jesus Christ, we can become, in the hands of almighty God, something new and useful. It is my hope that as you read this story of my personal journey as the founding pastor of Waterfront Church that you might be encouraged and challenged yourself to allow God to sand off your rough edges and reform your walk to make you look more like Christ. This is the call of every disciple. "He must become greater and I must become less." (John 3:30)

It is my prayer that your heart would transform into the likeness of Christ through your reading of this book. But, this book has a second purpose as well. In the midst of me giving my heart and my life to Christ and becoming a new creation, God called me to a new creation as well—to take part in something truly founded in faith shaped by the fingers of the Master. This was something invisible and at the time, nonexistent, that God had called me to in the midst of his grand creativity. In our case, we were called to start a church where one did not exist before, with people we had not yet met, in a place I had never been. The hands of

God have been evident throughout this process. The details had to be recorded so that the people of our church and our partner churches would not forget the beautiful path carved out by God in our church's early existence. It is my fervent hope that during this journey the Holy Spirit would prompt you, the reader, with dreams, ideas, and visions for God-sized tasks you, too, could never have imagined. It is my prayer that from this story you might find courage to deploy on the mission field, plant a local church, start a Christ-centered business, step up to teach the next generation how to defend the Gospel, or simply just say 'yes' to the really impossible stuff for the kingdom of God that could only come from His unmatched mind. For the most part, what you are about to read is a story about a Dad, his son, and the dream of starting a church in Washington, D.C., however you will also find entrepreneurial wisdom sprinkled throughout as well. Get ready for life in the hands of our creator!

Chapter 1:
Unlikely Monuments

I love hearing stories about companies or bands that began in someone's garage. Getting to see the humble beginnings of something that will later be viable, sustainable, and thriving is always so inspiring to me. It's a reminder, in many ways, that our God is the great creator and that his vast creative nature knows no bounds. What was one day just an ordinary neighborhood garage, when infused with vision and creativity, becomes an unlikely monument to where a movement began.

A studio apartment was the birthplace of the vision for Waterfront Church. In square footage, it is actually quite comparable to a garage. This was my studio where I lived while I finished out college in Stillwater, Oklahoma. It is beyond ironic that God gave me a vision to plant a church in Washington, D.C., in an apartment complex in Oklahoma called the "Presidential Studios." Each unit was named after a different president and I lived in "Washington 1A." As far as college living goes, it was a nice enough place. I was the first to live in my newly built unit, and I had no idea it would become a piece of holy ground for our story. The story of Waterfront Church begins with a simple prayer that I learned during my high school years. In fact, I believe that this prayer, when prayed with your whole heart, epitomizes the core of genuine discipleship. The prayer is simply: "God I'll do whatever you want me to do." No strings attached. No hooks. No buts. The old timers prayed Jesus's version, "thy will be done on earth as it is in heaven." This is not a hard prayer to pray, but it is a very hard prayer to mean.

My early days of praying this prayer could be marked by the conditions I gave God while praying it. I would pray, "God I'll do whatever you want me to do, as long as you let me date this particular girl, make this certain amount of money, or live in this particular place." No soldier offers their commanding officer conditions; they offer their allegiance. It took years for my heart to be prepared to give God the allegiance he was calling for, but everything came to a head during my senior year of college. I had not been living for Christ like I should have been up to that point and was very ashamed of the man I was becoming. However, I had recently experienced a spiritual awakening, and I was trying to seek the Lord with my whole heart.

At the time, I was being mentored by a youth minister named Derek Dennis (we called him coach because that had been his profession before doing ministry) at the First Baptist Church in Yukon, Oklahoma. It was a haul from Stillwater to Yukon, about an hour and a half each way but

I didn't care because I was growing so much in my faith in this ministry. The pastor at the church, a man named John Carey, had been my Dad's roommate in college and the Lord used him to foster a safe environment for me to confess my mistakes, make Godly friends, and learn to put Christ first over my own agenda. One day, I was serving as a sponsor on a youth ministry retreat and coach asked me a very pointed question: "Have you ever prayed all day before?" I was puzzled. I told him I prayed without ceasing like scripture says to in 1 Thessalonians 5:17, if that's what he meant. He expounded. "I mean, literally, have you ever given an entire day to God in prayer?" He went on to describe what a day like this might resemble: taking the day off from work, turning off the cell phone, and getting alone, just me and God. This idea was revolutionary for me, which is still surprising because it seemed like something I should have tried before this point. He then closed the discussion by telling me to make sure I told God I'd do whatever he wanted me to do.

So, on a very normal, unlikely day during my senior year of college I prayed the disciple's prayer for the very first time with my whole heart, soul, mind and strength. My girlfriend and I had just broken up, so that wasn't a hook. I was about to graduate from college and was willing to do any job, so that wasn't a hook. And I was honestly willing live anywhere, so that wasn't a hook. I just wanted God to give me direction so I could fulfill my purpose and be who he made me to be.

Jesus says to his Disciples in Luke 9, "If anyone would come after me, he must deny himself, take up his cross daily and follow me." We've got to die daily to our own agenda, and not just die, but PAINFULLY die via the cross. When we do that, we become alive in him! That day in prayer was life-changing. It was a little awkward at first, and there were definitely some points of silence, but what friendship doesn't have those if you spend a whole day together! I had been asking God all day what he wanted me to do with my life. I'd been telling him I would do anything he wanted, no conditions. And then, at the foot of my sagging futon in the Presidential studio apartments of Stillwater, Oklahoma, the Lord cast vision for people I had never met in and a place I had never been in Washington, DC. In the most ordinary of places, God was beginning an extraordinary journey.

Chapter 2:
Well-Placed Trust

Have you ever wanted a specific someone to respect you? Respect is definitely earned and not given, and some people's respect costs more than others. My entire life I wanted my Dad's respect. Dad was a powerful preacher, great with athletes and leaders, brilliant, funny, and, when I was a kid, I would just follow him around like a little puppy dog. He was my hero before I even knew what a hero was. Growing up, I got to see God establish unlikely spiritual monuments just about everywhere he went. Dad would later call this concept "leaving a shadow" the idea that you have lived as such a reflection of Christ that when people see places you've been or people you've interacted with, they are reminded of what God has done and give Him glory.

Dad left a lot of shadows. When I was in the 6th grade, Dad left the church he had been pastoring in Lubbock, Texas, for the field of full-time evangelism. For more than 20 years, he traveled the country sharing the Gospel and inspiring leaders. Let me be clear, he was not a perfect man by any stretch and my childhood was marked by some of the same bumps and bruises along the way that many other preacher's kids accumulate, but I had a great Dad. My Dad was a top-notch preacher and he was in high demand, so he was gone a lot and he missed some important milestones in my life. Thus, as I grew, so did some resentment. My Dad was always my hero, but when I got to college and drifted into a sinful lifestyle, the rift got even larger between Dad and me. He would never say it, but I'm certain he was deeply disappointed in me for my poor decisions. Gaining his respect seemed like an impossibility and so we didn't talk much through those years. To make matters worse, every time we were together, I would bring up every awful thing he had ever done to me in an attempt to gain closure.

The truth was that I had been using my Dad's shortcomings to justify my own sin and deflect the Holy Spirit's conviction. This is a pathetic cycle that a lot of believers fight against. You will be held accountable for you own life. Because of my constantly dredging up the past, Dad understandably avoided me like the plague and, looking back, I don't blame him. However, during my senior year, I was changing. I began to realize that my sin was not between me and my Dad, but it was between me and God. I awakened to the fact that I was wasting my life and was ineffective due to looking back when God had a glorious plan for my present and future.

So, on the night God gave the vision for Waterfront Church in Washington, D.C., I called my Dad for the first time in a long while. I was unsure of how to process what God had shown me. Just for the record, I grew up Southern Baptist. I had one vision, one time, because that's all my little Southern Baptist brain could handle! What I experienced was so intense and different that I wanted to reach out to another Godly leader to gain understanding, affirmation, and clarity in my circumstances.

So, I took a chance and called Dad and he answered! At first, when he picked up the phone, he was a bit caught off guard. He told me to slow down and tell him the story of how this vision from God came to be. I told him about Coach Derek and the day of prayer. I told him about seeing Washington, D.C., even though I had never been there. And then I told him the weirdest part. The vision concluded with God showing me an old man with a white beard standing next to a young man in a green shirt in the Capitol rotunda. These tiny details will prove of great importance later. There is no piece in a vision from God that is meant to be wasted. Dad listened, not saying a word through most of my description. It must have been perplexing to him. His son was describing this crazy God-proclaimed vision that had been given to a person that had only recently been living for Christ again.

I remember he listened to all of it before saying a word. His response was priceless. "First of all, don't tell anyone. Time will tell whether this was a vision from God or bad pizza." Ha! I still have to laugh at that. It was fantastic advice, especially coming from another Southern Baptist. Vision, sometimes, is meant to be contemplated and interpreted before it is proclaimed from the rooftops. Your vision was meant for you. Do not expect just anyone to understand and be smart enough not to cast the pearls of wisdom and creativity that God has given you before uninterested swine.

As I've gotten older, I've also come to the realization that there are some in this world who are unable to hear the creative voice of God, either because it is not their gifting to create or they have unconfessed sin blocking their ability to discern the voice of the Holy Spirit. When desperate, these people can attempt to hijack your vision and pawn it off as their own. In Christ, there should be no spirit of competition, but for the Godly leader to flippantly toss about the inner workings of their God-given vision before anything has come to fruition is reckless. Protect a word from God like you would a precious child. It's a great gift for you!

"Second," he said, "write everything down, just like Isaiah or Ezekiel." Any time God makes the effort to supernaturally guide your steps, you must have the presence of mind to record the message. No word from God is ever meant to be wasted. God's promises are also timeless. We write them down because what's true today with God will most certainly be true both tomorrow and forever. His holiness and purity requires it.

As our conversation ended, I wasn't sure if I was a step closer to Dad's respect or a step closer to the loony bin in his mind, but I know what I saw and I wanted to do whatever God wanted me to do, even at the expense of my Dad's respect. You see, God doesn't just want our relationship with him to be more important than our sin; he wants to be over ALL the good, the bad and the ugly. I had no idea as to the extent of the tapestry that God was weaving together that night. God had so many pieces working. Godly people in our lives are extremely important to our faith journey. They are sources of wisdom and insight, encouragement and caution, BUT, they are not God.

Most of the time in my walk with God, there is great unity and compatibility when it comes to the word of God and the advice of Godly people. However, God desires for his word and will to be most important voices we hear, even when it comes to our spiritual heroes. The words of Jesus in Luke 9 bounce in my brain when I remember this story, "he who would lose his life for my sake will find it." That night, at the Presidential studio apartments, I had pledged my allegiance to God in a way like never before. I had given him all of me. My sin, my plans, and even my goals, and in return, he gave me a vision– that would bless my life more than I ever could have imagined!

Chapter 3:
Waiting and Waiting

Have you ever seen lightning strike something in person before? Video doesn't do it justice. West Texas, where I grew up, and Oklahoma, where I went to college, are known for having some pretty spectacular lightning storms. I vividly remember sitting in my 12th floor dorm room watching clouds roll in with lightning shooting through them in all directions. Just breathtaking. Once, I was sitting on a porch in the country when lightning struck about a hundred feet from me near a tree. There was a massive explosion, sparks flew out from the tree, and the noise was so loud, my ears rang! What a moment! This is what I had expected a vision to be like. Loud, explosive and setting everything in my world on fire. Maybe even literally, but it wasn't.

Afterward, everything still seemed the same. I still had class and work on Monday. I still had questions about the future. And, honestly, God had given me a glimpse at my purpose, but no real concrete details of how to get there. But through the vision, I had learned the most important piece of the puzzle, I needed to daily tell God I would do whatever he wanted me to do. And through the process, a bunch of seemingly ordinary days serving the Lord, when grouped together, might just produce a truly extraordinary life and vision. Colossians 3:23 sums up how we should live while God is molding his new creation in and through us: "Whatever you do, do it with all your heart as you are working for God and not for men."

The Lord had redeemed me from the sin that so easily entangled me, and I was not going back. My experience with God was not as much like a lightning bolt, as it was a moment of resolute decision making. My life and my steps would belong to God now, and WHATEVER I did, I would do with all my heart for him. Just to be clear, I was still deeply flawed, imperfect, and broken, but I had given the controls to Christ and my main objective was to live for him. The attitude change would eventually affect our daily dealings as well. Too many times, we get caught up in correcting our bad behavior and we miss the attitude adjustment that will help us truly repent.

So, with this new Christlike attitude, I went back to what seemed like my old life, not knowing that God was doing something new! In the midst of my foolish college years, I had managed to do a couple of things right. I was making decent enough grades to keep my scholarship, and I had been working since the first semester of my freshman year at the finest restaurant in America, Red Lobster! While I was waiting for God's direction, I was also waiting on tables at the restaurant. And honestly, I loved it. Waiting tables is not for everyone or even for most people, but it was right up my alley. I like meeting new people, being helpful, and eating. It was a great match. And, the harder you worked, the more money you could make! However, the thought of waiting tables with a degree had me a bit concerned. Throughout the last semester of my senior year, I was scouring the internet for ministry jobs, and calling everyone I could think of that might be willing to hire me. One of those calls was to a man named John Strappazon.

"Strap" was the college minister at the First Baptist Church in Lubbock, Texas and someone who understood my story and family. He and my Dad had started a bible study 6 years earlier that had grown to around 1,600 college students on Thursday nights. Dad and Strap were quite a team. My Dad was the passionate preacher that would come in from the road and inspire the students and Strap was the steady hand of discipleship developing a pipeline of great commission fulfilling world changers. It was Holy Spirit magic to be around. When I got around to reaching out to Strap, he said he had been hoping I would call. This was a good sign! He said he would love to teach me how to disciple others in following Christ, BUT there was no position he could offer me or money he could pay me. The wind immediately left my sails. I had to make money. My student loans would start to kick in 6 months after graduation and I needed to know I had a source of income lined up. I was kind in the call, but I hung up the phone discouraged.

Why hadn't God provided a job for me? But, then I remembered that I already had a job waiting tables. It was not my calling or even an ideal use of my degree, but it did pay. And after 4 years of doing it, I could almost wait tables in my sleep. I knelt in prayer and told God, yet again, I'll do whatever you want me to do. There was no part of my life that was off limits to God, even my pride. Don't think it was easy selling the move back to Lubbock to my parents and friends. But,, I didn't care. I knew this was what God wanted me to do. And I was going to do it with my whole heart, no matter what people thought. So I moved to back to Lubbock, Texas, my hometown, to wait tables with a degree in hopes I could learn how to disciple. It still sounds crazy even as I type it, but it was a critical piece in the new creation God was beginning. His word tells us that his ways are higher than our ways, and my trek back to Lubbock days after graduation is a perfect reminder of that for me.

I pulled into town in the last week of December 2003. It was cold and windy, and I had no real place lined up to live. Thank God, my cousin Andy let me sleep on his couch that first night. I remember weeping when everyone in his house went to bed that night. I was realizing the weight of my sin from my wasted years in college, and I felt like coming back to Lubbock was a punishment or perhaps penance from

God to shame me. But, that's not how God works. He was not shaming me or rubbing my nose in my mistakes, he was humbling me and breaking me so that I would be prepared for his new creation. That night, I asked God for courage, sang songs of praise and then went to bed, praying myself to sleep, a practice I still utilize to this day when shame and fear seem to overtake me.

The next day, I went to Red Lobster and submitted a request for transfer. It was approved immediately, and I think I started working again that night. My grandparents on my Dad's side also lived in Lubbock and they offered their front bedroom to me while I figured things out, And my other grandmother, on my mom's side, offered to let me live in an efficiency my grandad had built in their backyard before he passed away. I'll always be grateful for them helping me. God had provided free living out of thin air so I could pay my student loan instead of rent.

That next week, I set up a time to see Strap for our first meeting. I felt like I was Saul meeting with Peter after his conversion. I was nervous and carrying a ton of baggage. Strap asked me if I'd go for a walk with him to the Texas Tech campus, just up the road and then he very simply asked me for my story. The first words out of my mouth were quite telling. "Before I tell you my story," I said, "you have to understand my Dad and what he did to me when I was younger." It was the same song and dance. Strap was so wise.

And filled with the Spirit. He fired back before I could even start. "I don't want to hear about your Dad. I asked about you. Are you ready to let God do something new in you?" I began to weep in the middle of the campus.

The Holy Spirit, through Strap, had called my bluff. I was leveled. I was ready for something new! Anything God wanted to do I was up for! Strap's next words were unexpected: "I believe God wants to heal your relationship with your Dad." Those were words I had longed for in the depths of my spirit to hear, but I was too afraid to utter them, even to the Lord. "How?" I asked, "I'll do anything." He said, to start, I was going to have to forgive him. Up until this point, I had been seeking an apology, not offering forgiveness. I asked him how this was possible, and he smiled and said to follow Christ's example. We love as Christ loved us. We forgive as Christ forgave us. Strap then pitched a concept. My Dad was still coming to Lubbock every Thursday to preach the college bible study. Strap offered the most simple and practical show of forgiveness ever.

He said, "Your Dad never eats before he preaches, and he loves (like any preacher) to hear that the Lord spoke through him during his message. What if you ran up to What-a-burger (if you've never been there, put down the book, schedule a flight and make it happen), got him a burger and fries just the way he likes them, handed him the food, told him something encouraging you got from

16

his message, and then walk away without blasting him for the past?" It was a revolutionary concept. Forgiveness in practical terms. It was worth a shot. When Thursday night came I was nervous. He preached amazingly as always, and there was a huge gathering of students around him after the service. I had gotten his burger and fries, and I had my compliment prepared to present. His eyes caught mine while I was a couple dozen feet away and the look on his face was strained. I saw him differently that night.

He was bracing for the impact of my typical pattern of rehashing the past. "Hey Dad, I'm sorry to interrupt, but I got this for you. I know you get hungry after you preach." I handed him the bag and fumbled through an encouraging reiteration of something Dad had just preached. The encounter was about three sentences long, and I closed with, "I'll see you next week." This was not a drop the mic interaction. There was no power play. Genuine forgiveness is draped in humility and servanthood. He was stunned. As I walked away, I could see him staring at the bag perplexed. Could it be that he longed for reconciliation too?

I looked forward to the next week and kept praying like mad that God would tear down the walls I had so hatefully built in my Dad's heart. It was during that week I told the Lord I would never again bring up what had happened in the past with my Dad. Ever. The old me was gone and the new me was coming. I had been forgiven and Christ was teaching me to forgive. The next week, I walked up with the bag, and I was armed with my compliment. This time, Dad wasn't flinching as I walked up. He almost looked like he was anticipating me. I handed him the bag, gave him my compliment and turned to walk away, but before I could go, he asked me if I'd stick around and take him to the airport.

His flight back to the Dallas area always left Lubbock just before 6 a.m., and he asked if I would take him to the airport. I couldn't believe it. God was healing a decade old hurt– through What-a-burger and a few kind words! When you give God your allegiance without any condition or strings attached, he can use anything to bring about his glorious plan! Anything! This became our regular Thursday night for a whole year, and it was only the beginning of what God was creating. The tears still fill my eyes as I recount this part of the story. It never would have happened if I had been too prideful to wait tables with a degree in my hometown.

Chapter 4:
The Tapestry

W hen I was a kid, my parents took me to the circus, and it was amazing! It was the first time I had ever seen an elephant, and I even got to ride one after the show. During the main performance, we watched acrobats and jugglers, lions and giraffes, so many unforgettable sights. As a kid, I was seeing all of this for the very first time and my world was expanding.

In between each act, the clowns would come out to distract the crowd so that the next act could set up. One of their segments was the famous plate-spinning act. One extremely hard-working clown came out with a stack of plates and a collection of sticks. As pressure-inspired music filled the circus tent, the clown took the plates and one by one put them on individual sticks making sure to keep all new and old plates spinning. The mood was tense, and the audience had the sense that at any moment all the plates will come crashing down. Sometimes, when we think of God being in control of all things in our universe, we picture something to the effect of the clown feverishly spinning the plates. He is tense, frantic, and at any point, a neglected plate could fall and break. This could not be further from the truth. God is not just in control, he is sovereign. He cannot be stopped, thwarted, or deterred. He is all powerful, all consuming, and all good.

God's work is less like a clown spinning plates and more like a weaver of a fine and massive tapestry. Each thread in a tapestry is meticulously plotted and set. It works on multiple levels, seen and unseen. The tapestry is beautiful and complex, but void of chaos and disorder. A tapestry is stunning at a distance and quite different, but equally as impressive at close proximity. A tapestry tells a story and it must be durable. The artist must be equally creative and capable. God has a master plan for all things and is fully aware and concerned with every aspect of our individual existence. He is also creative and capable. And, he is the giver of joy and peace in the midst of chaos.

In Psalm 139, we get the description of God as having us surrounded. There is no where we can go where he is not. In sticking with the tapestry example, he even proclaims that he "knit" us together in our mother's womb. You see, God is not distant; he is very near, always. For anyone blessed with a vision from God for something new that does not yet exist, there will be stretches where it seems that the process has stalled when in truth, much is going on beneath the surface. The God of heaven sees every twist and turn and is bringing all things into alignment so that the glorious moment of creation can begin. It is a requirement that you understand that God's hands are guiding the process. Timing must belong to him. It is too important to be entrusted to our control.

So, what do you do while you wait? Live your life for Christ! The answer seems too simple. Shouldn't it be more complicated? Aren't there plates to spin? Remember, it is a tapestry, not a clown show that God is master of. Every person given a vision for a new creation must understand this principle: a vision from God is an amazing, heavenly gift with major ramifications for your life, but it in no way redefines your ultimate calling to love your God with all your heart and to make disciples until there is no breath left in your body.

The vision doesn't change you. Your walk of faith and your relationship with Christ changes you. The visionary must come to the realization that they would love and follow Christ even if there was no vision. Knowing him is the great reward! This portion of the journey can be a bit lonely because no one else can work on your heart but Christ. There is no visible timetable for this that human minds can comprehend and there is no checklist to complete, transcript to format, or network to build that proves you are worthy to get started. This phase depends on 3 major factors: how clearly you hear the Spirit, how quickly you obey, and how much control you are willing to let God have.

The year I moved to Lubbock after college was the year I fell head over heels in love with the Lord. The vision he had given was special, but the vision was not my reason for pursuing God. My relationship with God had become something so real and precious to me. It was just like David wrote in Psalm 63: My soul thirsts for you and my body longs for you like one in a dry and weary desert." That stretch was the first time I would wake up in the morning, think about spending time with God, memorize verses in between my shifts at work, pray with any friend throughout the day that would let me, and fall asleep for the night with my face in the scriptures after hours of reading and prayer. God's word came alive! His love for me leapt from the page, and my heart was full. I could see his hand at work all around me. And in those beautiful moments of intimacy, God began to reveal insecurities in my heart that needed to die.

Namely, that I hated being alone. It had created a pattern of jumping at relationships to fill the void, and that was keeping me from ever finding my forever relationship and, most importantly, finding my identity in Christ. You see, a lot of people say that they place their self-worth in their relationship with Christ, but loneliness still batters and beats their life with extreme efficiency. I'm not saying that there aren't periods of darkness that won't attempt to derail you, but for a heart intimately seeking Christ, there must come a moment of realization that you are never alone! God is always there with you, and he will be there for eternity. God must BE enough for you because he IS enough for you.

This is the moment that the visionary must realize that God's plans are not the reward; knowing Him is the reward! The old timers sang it this way: "Turn your eyes upon Jesus, look full in his wonderful face, and the things of earth will grow strangely dim in the light of his glory and grace." He is Enough. Any blessing, vision, relationship, testimony, or experience are simply gifts from heaven to enhance your relationship with the Almighty. This changes everything. The world seems to change shape. During this stretch, I was single and not dating anyone, but I never referred to myself as being alone. God was with me. He loved me like no one else ever could, and he sought me out even in the midst of my sin. He saw me as useful enough to give a vision. His word was new every day. And I was joyful for the first time in my life.

If you haven't figured it out yet, this is the ultimate new creation. You. And the intimacy you learn is available to you through knowing your creator. After a meeting with almighty God, you change, and it lasts for eternity. God becomes visible in and around your life, and if you can trust him, he will fill you and eliminate the gaping void in your soul. Peace unexplainable. Joy incomparable. Love undeniable. Purpose unlimited. Christ completes you. This is why, no matter the outward success or failure of your new creation, we find our purpose and meaning as we seek the Lord.

Chapter 5:
Sharing the Vision

Through the first year and a half, I had not told many people at all about my vision for D.C. partially because I didn't understand what it meant, and mostly because I was afraid that people would laugh at me or think I was weird. A vision for something new is so precious, but it is also so fragile. The enemy knows that the confidence and momentum needed to get something started can be easily stifled right out of the gate.

Even the fastest runners in the world can lose a race because of an awful start. I was doing my best to trust the Lord in my walk with him, but I longed for a ministry partner. Someone I could share every detail with, that would offer Godly counsel, that would intercede for me and not think I was crazy, and that would be up for this journey together. That's when I met my wife, Autumn. Just for the record, this person does not have to be your spouse. It is not bad or weak to pray for a spiritual partner in your new creation venture. It's actually highly biblical.

Jesus consistently sends the disciples out in twos to carry his message to the villages. Two can encourage one another in times of difficulty or persecution. Two can sharpen one another in times of confusion or theological wandering. Two can rejoice together on the best days and weep together on the unthinkable ones. When it comes to your new creation, remember, it is not good for man to be alone. Autumn was serving as the girl's intern for the college ministry at our church in Lubbock. There were more than a 1,000 college students, and she was the only girl's intern. She was the best of the best. She was well spoken and gave the announcements each week in the service in addition to leading a small group. In her spare time between class and ministry, she gave campus tours at Texas Tech University. Her smile was infectious, and the love of Christ was all over her life. She smiled so often that her eyes had a natural squint to them, telling the world that her joy was not fleeting, but a defining characteristic woven into her being and her unwavering love for her savior. I was smitten. I still am.

We went on our first date on March 2, 2004 and were married less than a year later on January 15, 2005. The day I told her about the vision I was filled with insecurity. We were just dating at that point, and I didn't want to scare her off by sounding like a lunatic. It is at this point that the refiners process from the previous chapter is so important. Like I said, I was smitten with this girl. I wanted to marry her, almost from the first month we were dating. But, in order for me to fulfill my calling as a disciple, I had to love God just a little bit more.

It's moments like this that you have to be honest about your new creation. Was it truly a God-given vision or was it just a good idea? I was not about to risk what was budding with Autumn over a good idea, but a God-given vision and the fact that I had given God my life, well, that was something I had to be honest about. This was more than just sharing a vision, this was letting her know that Christ comes first in my life and that the same would need to be true for anyone I marry. With nervousness and worry, I shared the vision with Autumn. Her response shined out in her eyes before a word left her lips. She kindly listened. She reaffirmed the work of God in my life. She took in the details and said she thought it sounded amazing. Something stirred in me. I wondered if she had experienced a vision like this before, and maybe it was about D.C. too!

I'm not sure what I was expecting in that moment. Maybe that she would say she had had the same vision. Maybe that she would say she had been praying for D.C. since she was a child. There was no telling. I asked her the question and received an important response. "No, I've never had a vision like that, and I'd never thought of doing ministry in D.C. until today, but I do believe God gave you this vision and I want to help." I wasn't let down by her answer and it teaches a very powerful point that each visionary must embrace.

A true vision from God is ultimately between you and God. On your journey toward the new creation, God is going to send you partners and encouragers, but they will almost certainly come along without the benefit of experiencing the same vision you have. This means two things: the visionary must run to God for intimacy and understanding above all others because he is the only one who truly understands, and the visionary must be patient with their partners because the partner's journey is different than the visionary.

And then there were two. Waterfront Church in Washington, D.C., had just gotten its first family and we didn't even know it!

Chapter 6:
With My Own Eyes

As a kid growing up in Texas, I always remember wondering what it would be like to go to New York City. Countless movies, TV shows, and songs do their best to explain and give you a taste of the experience. The sound of the taxi's, the flow of the pedestrians, the tone of the New York accent, the look of the buildings ... artists do their very best to capture it, but there is truly no comparison to your first time seeing the city in person. I had just turned 21 when I went to New York City for the first time.

I flew into JFK and then caught a cab straight to Times Square at about 9 p.m. in the beginning of June. It was just after dusk, about 75 degrees, and no breeze. As I got out of the cab I thought my brain was going to explode! The buildings were even bigger than I had imagined. The lights were brighter, and the sounds were louder. There were more people than I had ever seen anywhere at one time. There was stuff going on all night and into the morning without a break in the action. It was beautiful! After you see New York City in person it even changes the way you watch movies about New York City. I no longer was limited to secondhand knowledge of the city; I had seen it with my own eyes, observed it with my own mind, smelled it with my own nose, and that experience changed things.

There was a major issue when it came to my D.C. vision that needed to be remedied as soon as possible such as the fact that I had never been there! Not even for an academic trip. It is one of the reasons why the vision was so interesting. God had cast vision for a people I had never met and a place I had never been. Flying in from Texas was expensive and, as we would learn later, it was a 26-hour drive from where we lived to D.C. This was not just an easy jaunt East. It was going to take a hefty commitment even to visit, and for a new couple that couldn't even afford a couch, flying to D.C. seemed like a distant dream.

Right after Autumn and I got married, I took a job as the student minister at First Baptist Church in Grapevine, Texas, while I was attending Seminary. I was very young, so young in fact, that my first year there I was too young to even drive the church van! You had to be 25 to be on the church's insurance. In one of my very first meetings at the church with my new pastor, Mike Mowery (a dear friend to this day), he informed Autumn and I that part of the job was planning a yearly mission trip for the students. "Where to?" I asked, not expecting his answer. "Anywhere the Lord leads," was his response.

As soon as we got home, Autumn was looking up ministry opportunities in D.C. for us to partner with. I was finally going to see it! So, later that summer, with leaders that were of legal age to drive the vans, we headed to D.C. with a team of 42. One of those joining us was a 16-year-old boy, Brad Morris, who would end up being a Waterfront Church deacon one day. More on him later. Washington, D.C. was different. Beautiful, but very different from TV and the movies. I had never seen homelessness like this before. There were people in need everywhere you looked. My ears also heard a wider variety of languages than ever before. This was a global city, and the people here were driven by a sense of ambition that I had never known before. Ambition to stay for those who grew up here. Ambition to make it here for those from somewhere else. And beneath the polished surface was a deep lust for power and purpose like nowhere else in the world.

The vision became more complicated the day that we arrived in the city simply because I felt ill equipped for the task set before me. Questions began to swirl around in my head. I had grown up in suburban Texas. How could I lead an inner-city ministry? I was a B student in a city of straight A students. Didn't God have someone smarter to do this? The needs in this city were so great; what possible difference could one person make? Remember, friends, the easiest place for the enemy to disrupt are a few steps from the starting blocks. John writes for us in 1 John 4, "greater is he that is in me than any power that's in this world."

That means that if you have Jesus Christ, you win. It doesn't matter how deep, dark, difficult, and frightening the world becomes ... if you have Jesus, you win. This means that, for the believer, the Devil cannot defeat you. Thanks be to God who gives us the victory in Christ Jesus! But the devil has been around a long time and he has a couple of tricks. If you have Christ and the devil can't beat you, it becomes his goal to distract and discourage you. These tricks seem powerful, especially for someone pursuing a new creation that does not yet exist. But I assure you, the enemy only has the power and influence that we allow him to have. So, how do we fight through distraction and discouragement on our way to our God-given vision? I'll make it as simple as possible ... time in the presence of God. Perfect love casts out fear. Find time and reason daily to get alone with God and let him restore your faith and erase your fear.

This happened on the Wednesday night of our mission trip. We had just spent the day feeding, clothing, and preaching to the homeless in D.C. We met some amazing people, some of them believers who wept as they told our students their stories of how they ended up on the street. Our hearts were broken for these people and this city. That night, we gathered for prayer and to sing songs of worship at the Star of Bethlehem Church in Northwest D.C. where we were staying. Our worship leader that night was would end up being Waterfront Church's first worship leader almost a decade later. That night, I walked up in front of the students to start the service and asked the students to pray for D.C., the people they had met, and for the things God had planned for the city in the future. I then told the worship leader to play some background music on his guitar and when the kids stopped praying, then he could start leading the group in songs of worship.

What happened next was special. The kids began to pray. And pray. And pray. And the prayers kept increasing in volume. Not yelling or fiery, just louder with power. Kids and adults were weeping. Autumn and I were weeping. About 15-20 minutes passed and he began to sing in worship, but there was no sound system and you could not even hear his guitar. He finally just set the guitar down and joined the people praying. They prayed for hours. It was unbelievable. I had never experienced anything like it before. The Holy Spirit had fallen on the room of 42. The vision had been reaffirmed and now everything was going to change. A new creation requires the supernatural. We do not have the ability to create something from nothing. Only God has that power. We can reform, manipulate, or fashion something that already exists, but only God can create something from nothing. A true moment of consecration is extremely powerful when it happens on site. What had started as a day of insecurity and fear had become an understanding that maybe, just maybe, God had made me for such a time and a task as this. That night the Lord added 2 more to the Waterfront team, our worship leader and Brad, without our knowing, almost a decade before the church's first service. And then there were 4.

Chapter 7:
Pay the Price

When I was a kid, I enjoyed playing sports of all kinds. I was what a tactful person might call an "energetic child," and my mother said the nursery workers had lovingly nicknamed me "kid destructo." Athletics were a way for my busy, creative mind to burn off energy. Basketball and baseball were fun, but football became a true passion for me. It is the ultimate team sport. No one person can win by themselves. In baseball, a pitcher can almost single-handedly dominate the opposition. In basketball, one person can dominate on offense and defense if they are talented enough.

But in football, the game is too rough, exhausting and complicated for one person to carry the load. The player's ability might be celebrated, but they cannot win alone. Football taught me how to depend on others, how to take a hit and get back up again, how to celebrate and encourage the men bleeding next to me in our struggle for victory, how to navigate my emotions through victory and defeat, and how to win the respect of my teammates through hard work, dedication, and consistency in my walk with Christ.

The Apostle Paul lays out the path to victory for the athlete and the believer in 1 Corinthians 9 when he writes "Do not all runners run in a race but only one receives the prize? Run in such a way as to get the prize." Athletes don't just run, they run to win! Paul goes on to say that for this reason, an athlete goes into "strict training to gain a perishable wreath, but we do so to gain a crown that lasts forever." In order for the athlete to win, training is a requirement before entering the race. When it comes to our new creation, God is very concerned with us being as prepared as possible for his vision. Let me chase that statement with a famous statement: God does not call the qualified, he qualifies the called. It is important to remember that you did not receive your vision from God because you are good or have earned it, but rather the vision has come because God, in his great mercy, chose to send you a vision. However, once given the vision, we MUST be good stewards of the deposit entrusted to us and begin training our hearts for our upcoming deployment. In football, that strict training was two-a-day practices the week before school started. Let me be clear, every athlete lives for game day! Nobody in their right mind values practice over the game. Practice is meant to benefit the game!

Spiritually, this would be like a person studying spiritual disciplines but never actually applying them in their life. It is foolishness. But, also destructive is a person that goes into a game situation having missed practice all week. Spiritually, this is a person striving to live for Christ without any of God's word hidden in their heart. Their life will be undisciplined, confusing to onlookers, and ripe with avoidable mistakes. The first day of practice is seemingly the most uneventful. That day, we reported to the field house to be fitted for pads and to have our physical examination. This was a day filled with cutting up and messing around because we just stood in line with our friends for hours.

How was this training? Didn't we have better things to do? On the contrary, this day was critical. These were the pads we would wear every day for the rest of the season. They would protect our limbs, head and muscles from injury. And if they did not fit properly, we would be right back in that fitting room later in the season getting help. The physical examination was even more important. This is the time we found out if we were even fit for play. On more than one occasion, the seemingly uneventful physical revealed a major issue with teammates of mine that needed immediate medical attention. One of my friends had developed a heart murmur that his physical examination revealed. He could have died out there under the wrong circumstances.

Very rarely will God give you a vision that places you immediately in a game-day environment. If you have time to receive training, use it! If you have a moment for spiritual self-reflection, use it! Allow God to prepare your heart for deployment. A new creation is not something we can see just yet, so you have no idea what you are up against or even a crystal-clear picture of what you are working towards. But God does! Let him coach you so that you are ready for game time. The next day of two-a-days were the worst. Conditioning. This was the moment you realized how out of shape you were after a glorious summer of video games, junk food and late nights. No one was ready for this day not even the ones who prepared. Perseverance and endurance were the virtues on display during conditioning day, and every year, we saw talented guys quit on the first day. I can still hear Coach Roy Phelps and Cory Barnes, my defensive coaches yelling, "Pay the price men! Pay the price!"

Paul outlines Conditioning Day in 1 Corinthians 9 as well. Paul writes, "I beat my body and make it my slave so that after I have preached to others, I might not be disqualified for the prize." Perseverance and endurance keep us from losing the blessings that Come with God's glorious new creation. We must be conditioned to listen to the Holy Spirit and not the burning desires of our flesh. The hardest part of conditioning day was also the realization that this was not something we would do once and be done with it. We would continue conditioning until the final play of our season was run. Such is the life of the believer.

The training we go through for the sake of the Gospel is meant to be replicated day after day, situation after situation. Don't quit! Pay the price, friend! Pay the price! After conditioning, we began learning offensive and defensive plays. Quarterback running backs and receivers worked on their timing, ball control, and footwork. Lineman worked on identifying defenses and memorizing protections. And my group, the defense, worked on reading and reacting to the offense's movements, plugging gaps, and form tackling. I can't help but grin as I type this portion of the story. I loved every minute of football. It was during this phase that the season would begin to take shape. We learned plays and developed a game plan. We learned to trust each other, and we developed muscle memory we would need later during the games. We came together as a team.

If God has you in a time of training before your new creation takes life and your vision becomes a reality, know that there must be something big in store! Our God does not waste time. If you are ready, he'll send you. Our God wants us to be "lacking nothing and equipped for every good work" (James 1). And you never know what blessings will reveal themselves during a period of training that will be absolutely critical later.

It's another story for another day, but I went through a deep time of trial and training while I was on staff at a church in North Central Texas. It was very similar spiritually to the conditioning day described above. Endurance and perseverance were being cultivated in my heart by the Holy Spirit, and my pride was being eliminated at an accelerated pace. And believe me, my pride had developed into quite the vicious beast over the years. I had just returned from what would end up being the final mission trip we would lead to D.C. before moving there to start our church almost 5 years later. It was at that time that my wife and I found the courage to resign out of principle and abandon what was truly for us a toxic ministry environment without having another job. I had never really quit anything in my entire life. It was humiliating however, it was also during that time that God revealed that I had tied so much of my self-worth into what my job title was. To make matters heavier, our first child, Lulu, was only 4 months old, and she had been born with some breathing complications. This was tough conditioning.

As a side note, if any of you are considering quitting your job without another job secured, I beseech you, do not even think about it unless the Lord is clearly telling you to do so. It is so hard. Quitting without another job in place affected me and my family for more than a year after the decision, but because the Lord had called for it, we followed his leading. A week after quitting, I was sitting at dinner with my mom and Dad, my wife, Autumn, and daughter, Lulu, on a Wednesday night in Frisco, Texas. It was a delicious Tex-Mex restaurant called "Manny's" that served an all-you-can-eat buffet on Wednesdays only. Up until then, I had never eaten the special buffet because I served in student ministry and always had preached on Wednesday nights. Needless to say, I was feeling inadequate to say the least.

Half-way through the meal, a man walks up and starts a conversation with my Dad. Apparently, he and Dad had worked together in the past. After some small talk, he asks my Dad, "What are you doing now, Jon?" Dad offers an answer and then follows suit by asking the same question back to the man, "What are you doing now?" It was in that moment that I felt my heart beating so fast that I thought my chest was going to cave in, just like the conditioning day during the first week of two-a-days. I couldn't breathe, and I ran outside to the parking lot and knelt in the gravel. I was emotional. My wife retrieved the baby carrier and headed out after me. "What's wrong?" she asked, deeply concerned for what would make me behave this way. "I don't do anything," I told her. "If he had asked me what I did, I couldn't say anything!" My loving wife and ministry partner wrapped her arms around me, prayed for me and encouraged me that we had done the Lord's will. It was right there in the gravel parking lot of Manny's in Frisco, Texas, that another unlikely spiritual monument, just like the one at the Presidential Studios in Stillwater, Oklahoma, formed. I told the Lord that day that I was his, no matter my title, my salary, or my perks. Like the beautiful worship song by Tim Timmons says, "I praise you, not that I have to, and not that I ought to, but that I may."

It was in that parking lot that my pride was put to death, brutally and without mercy. We would later learn that an excess of pride in D.C. provides for swift destruction. It had to go for the new creation to flourish. Just days after that moment in the parking lot, I got a call from a church that I never would have considered working for to be their discipleship pastor. The church was only 6 years old, was located in my hometown of Lubbock, Texas, and it already had a bit of an unstable reputation. But, let me tell you, this church would end up being precious to Autumn and me, as well as an incubator for a mind striving to learn how to plant a church. My Dad was the first voice of affirmation for the job.

At first I thought he was just worried I'd never get another offer, but he told me this church was special, that God was moving there and that I needed to see it firsthand before I made a judgement. The night before we visited, Autumn and I drove to the church to survey the scene. It was so small compared to the church we had come from. The lobby at our former church was bigger than this church's entire facility! Pride attempted to rear its ugly head, but it could find no foothold. I was strong in my weakness and the Lord was guiding our steps. God was ready to open the floodgates of blessing in my life through this church, and I can honestly say it took the pride- murdering experience of quitting a job to prepare my heart to say yes to going there.

The church was called Victory Life and let me tell you that, for our family, it was perfectly named because we could not have felt more defeated at that point. So, we loaded our four-month-old and attended the church service and it was a crazy experience. The Holy Spirit was there, and my heart was broken for whatever God would ask for. In the middle of the singing portion of the service, as we were crying out to God, an amazing truth hit me: the church plant was not the only new creation God was working on; I was becoming a new creation too! The old me was gone and the new me, the Christlike me, was starting to be shaped and crafted for the Lord's will. Again, I was very emotional.

You see, in order for God to start something new through you, he must create something new in you. At the end of the service, the pastor (Brad Jurkovich, a dear friend and ministry partner), announced to the audience that there was a young man in the congregation with a heart for Washington, D.C. He was trying to sell me on the job at Victory Life. He asked the congregation to pray for my family, for D.C. and then he dismissed the service. Autumn, Lulu and I left the church preparing to accept the job the next day, just 4 days before losing our medical benefits. We praised God in the car on the drive back to my grandparent's house where we were staying, having no clue that God was still at work at his divine potter's wheel.

At the end of the service, a rancher with a perfectly trimmed white mustache made his way to Pastor Brad. He asked the pastor who the young man was with a heart for Washington, D.C. The pastor replied that I had already left and that this had been my first Sunday at the church. The man smiled and said, "This is my first Sunday here as well, and I live half the year in Washington, D.C."

This man was David Godfrey, Waterfront Church's first board member. I'm writing this part of the book in a Starbucks, and tears flood my eyes as I recount this moment. As I was broken, spiritually gassed, and seemingly empty, God was making good on his promise to see the vision through to completion. A few days later, David and I met up for the very first time. This would be the first of a hundred. He asked about why we felt called to D.C., where we felt the Lord's leading to plant, and when we were planning to plant the church. At this point, God had not even given us the name yet. David's demeanor is a lot like a calculated detective when he is figuring someone out. I told him everything, including my crazy vision story down to the last detail. I told him about the area near the Navy Yard metro stop and the Nationals' ballpark that was serving as our target zone, and I told him we had to see this vision through. He was silent almost the entire first part of the meeting, just taking in information, but never revealing his emotions. I asked him what he thought, thinking there was a pretty high probability that he would just wish me good luck and leave.

Instead, David smiled. He said, "Did you know I've been prayer walking that area for almost a decade?" He told me that he had been working as an attorney and a consultant for various large projects and that the overhaul of the Navy Yard neighborhood in D.C. had been a key location he was researching. God had provided a true insider for us so that we could learn the flow of the city. God had provided our first spy in the land.

David began to coach me on the practical parts of site selection, a critical but often undervalued part of church planting. The Spirit of God can work anywhere, but it can hinder longevity and momentum for a new creation if people cannot find, get to or know the location of your gatherings. David is a dear friend and mentor. And then there were 5. Your training days do not have to be characterized by discouragement. It can actually be a time when God assembles and crafts the core of the new creation, starting with your own heart.

Chapter 8:
Developing Your Strategy

Let's look back before we look forward. For a kid, there are plenty of places that, for a short time, are off limits. Big kids and adults seem to have all the fun. Was there ever something in your life that you longed to be older so that you could do it? The first time I remember feeling this way was when I would see my grandads go out to their workshops in their backyards. You could not go there on your own. You had to be invited by grandad and even that wouldn't happen until you had proven yourself to be mature enough to handle what went on in the workshop. For years, I would play in the yard around the workshop and hear the squeal of saw blades, the clanging of hammers, with gospel music for one grandad and jazz music for the other, serenading the whole project. The music came from speakers that had themselves been built in the workshops at one point. Later that evening, the men would emerge with their spoils of victory, their new creation, if you will. As we sat around the table for dinner, I remember seeing an unparalleled look of satisfaction on grandad's face. The food tasted that much sweeter to him, and his mind was racing with thoughts of what the next project would be.

I had to figure out a way to get into that workshop! Finally, during 2nd grade, an opportunity arrived. The school I went to was doing an optional science fair. That word optional is key. I wanted to go into the workshop so badly, that I voluntarily took on more homework! I approached my grandad, Robert Earl Dennis, with the question—would he help me build something special for the fair? He was a printer by trade, and one of the godliest men I've ever known. He proudly said yes, and I began walking to the workshop with a spring in my step. "Hold your horses, young man, we are not headed in there just yet. This project begins at the kitchen table."

I was confused. I didn't care what the project was, I just wanted to get started in that workshop, with the noise and all the excitement. My disappointment was evident, so grandad was quick to clarify. "You have committed to a project, but you need to make your plan of action. Now, what do you want us to create together?" In that moment, he pulled out two small flip pads and two number 2 pencils. He kept a set for himself and handed a set to me. He then flipped to a clean sheet of paper in his note pad, licked the tip of the pencil, and looked into my eyes hoping to catch my vision for the project. It was kindness on a level I had not experienced before. He not only cared about what I was about to say, but he was genuinely listening to me—a man in his seventies, listening to a kid—AND he was taking notes!

I think my first response was based in fear. "What do YOU want to build?" I asked sheepishly. I had responded to his question with another question, but really I was telling him I just wanted to be around him and around his workshop. Grandad smiled and said, "Young man, this is YOUR project, and I need to know what YOU want to make. What would you be proud to take to that science fair?" My brain was racing a mile a minute, sprinting from idea to idea, and in the heat of the moment, I blurted out, "Can we build a telephone?"

Grandad adjusted his glasses and wrote something on the note pad. "Hmm," he said, "I like that thinking. A telephone would certainly be exciting, but I'm not sure I have the capabilities in my workshop to make that happen today. What made you choose a phone as the subject of our project?" This was an interesting question. As I remembered back, it turns out this was not such a random idea. "Well, at school, we have been studying about Alexander Graham Bell, and how we moved from the telegraph to the telephone." "Really?" He responded. He again adjusted his glasses, licked his pencil and wrote on the flip pad. "Now, there's an idea!" His eyes filled with life. "Yes, we could do that!" He flipped to a clean sheet and began to sketch.

I remember thinking, "What just happened?" I had just witnessed the birth of a project, a vision for our new creation but I had no idea what it was! After about 5 minutes of staring over his shoulder as he sketched, I finally got the courage to ask him, "Grandad, what are we making?" His entire being came to a halt. He looked me in the eyes, puzzled, and said, "A telegraph, of course! I have all the tools to make this right here my shop. Have a look at these drawings." Now his note pad was making sense. Grandad begins to tell me that during his time in World War II, he worked as a submarine trainer and that they had been given a background in understanding telegraphs because Morse code was so prevalent in Navy communication. I'd never heard him talk about that time in his life. In fact, even as I got older, he rarely talked about that time, but there I was, hearing the stories and formulating our strategy. We put together a list of materials we would need, including all the wiring and a light bulb for each telegraph station. The telegraph would make noise, but he said that the light would give the project some historical accuracy. I went with it. This was so much fun!

We got into his tiny Ford Ranger pickup truck and went to a local hardware store called Builders Square in Lubbock, Texas. Grandad was nodding to people he knew as we walked through the store. I was so proud to be with him. Some even asked what we were building. "I'm working for my grandson today," grandad would say, looking to see my response. "He doesn't pay much, but he's got some great ideas." I would blush and look at the floor. His friends would chuckle and move on. Again, I was so proud to be with him. We gathered our materials, grandad paid, and then we drove back to the workshop. I finally got to enter the promised land! It was amazing! Tools were everywhere! Gadgets and widgets hanging on the walls captured my attention. Grandad even had a barbed wire collection hanging over his work bench. And every tool had R.E.D. written on the handle, my grandad's initials, to let anyone who borrowed them know where to return them. He was so cool.

This was all I had dreamed of! After we unloaded the truck, grandad said, "Ok, let's head back to the kitchen table." I was stunned. "Why? We just got here!" Again, he smiled and said, "Young man, we still have some research to do before we get started." He led me back inside the house to his back bedroom. This was the room that held his favorite orange chair. Grandad was short, but quite round at this point in his retirement, and had bottomed out the springs in the chair's base so it was the most comfortable place on the planet to sit. Next to his chair was a shelf of Louis L'Amour books he would read in the evenings before bed as well as a set of huge Encyclopedia Britannica's. He pulled out the "letter T" book and flipped to the telegraph page. We read it together, gaining an historic understanding of what we were building and its original purposes, its successes, failures, and how it paved the way for modern day phones. Hearing my grandad read this is still burned into my memory. When he finished, he placed the book back into its rightful spot and said, "Ok, it's time to get to work."

We went back to the workshop better prepared for our project. Our strategy was clear, and everything was coming together. And, finally, I heard the words I'd been waiting my whole life to hear. "Zack, would you like to use the saw with me?" The saw?! Yes, yes, a thousand times yes! Only real construction people got to use the saw! So, of course, I played it cool. "Sure, I guess if you want me to." Grandad said, "We need to get an exact measurement on this piece. Use your tape measure first." I pulled out the tape measure from n my workshop assistant apron, and measured the piece, marking exactly where the cut needed to go. After that I set the board onto the cutting table and waited for my grandad to come over. "Measure it again," He called out. He had not even looked at it. "I already did," I barked back at him. "Measure it again," grandad called out again. "Measure twice, cut once." Wisdom. Deep wisdom. There are certain things in this life that once you do them, cannot be undone, like cutting a piece of wood too short. Measure twice, cut once. More on that in a minute.

I followed his directions and then called for him again. This time, he walked over, placed his hands on mine, and we cut the wood piece together. He was guiding the process but using my hands to do the work. More on that later as well. When the project was done, we went inside for dinner covered in sawdust and wire grease. The food tasted that much sweeter, and my mind was racing toward new projects I could undertake after conquering this new creation. He was proud of me that day. I could see it in his face. I already knew he loved me, but that day I knew with certainty that he was proud of me. Grandad would pass away my freshman year in college. He was the first person in our family that I remember dying that I knew well. After he died, I always wondered what happened to all of his tools. He had 5 children, including my mom, and I always assumed that the tools went to them, and some of them did.

The end of this little story is special. Three years after he died, I graduated from college and went back to Lubbock and served at my grandad's old church, First Baptist Church. That spring break we went on a construction mission trip to California and assisted in remodeling and erecting churches. The group we took was almost 300 college students and leaders, and it was a really neat trip. This was the trip that Autumn, my soon to be wife, was on as well, when we had only been dating for a few weeks. The site I was working on was rebuilding the church's stage, and at one point I was underneath it and had to ask to be passed tools from the community tool box. Construction will always remind me of my grandad. I can't remember if I was thinking of him in that moment under the stairs or not, but I do know he was on my mind a lot that week, especially when I measured for the second time before cutting anything. All of the sudden a hammer is slid under the stage to me with R.E.D. blaring on the handle. I cried. He had donated his tools to the mission work being done in churches on the West coast. I'll never forget God using my grandad in moments like this one, even after he had been dead for years. And, I'll never forget the lessons of how to formulate a strategy before jumping headlong into a new creation.

Don't be afraid of research. It is a complicated thing to get started after having a God-given vision. You can almost feel like gathering information is a sign of faithlessness, but the opposite is actually true. Research is often a source of reaffirmation of the vision. Think about the spies going into the promised land for the first time. They were fearful of the task ahead, but saw a land filled with milk and honey. Their research reaffirmed that God's plan was good, and that his promise was going to be better than advertised. Sadly, their research also revealed a few more problems, too (giants in the land, etc.), and all but two of the spies said to hold off on the move. As we have reiterated before, pursuing a new creation is not for the faint of heart or the weak of stomach. You must be willing to know what you are getting yourself into first so you can formulate your plan, and second, so you can fully realize just how miraculously the hand of God was present through your process.

When planting our church, we went straight to the web site census.gov to gather demographics on our target area in D.C. We wanted to know who we were being called to reach, and just how plentiful the harvest could be. Let me just tell you, our neighborhood, the Navy Yard, was a land of milk and honey. It was made up of small houses that were less than a mile from the Capitol building that were being replaced by high-rise condos. Tens of thousands of people would be moving within feet of the church. The area was going to be diverse economically, racially, and in age distribution. We began to see what God sees: people in need that we could actually know how to help! Oh yeah, there were giants, too. The area is one of the most expensive places to live and work in the entire United States, and it would just about take an act of God, or Congress (pun intended) to get a meeting space. But, the research was clear that this could work. Better yet, this had the potential to be a historic ride! Do you have the courage to gather information on you project? Do you have thick enough skin to allow God to reshape your project if the data reveals a different need? God will not ask you to walk blindly into your life's purpose. He encourages the faithful. However, if you don't do the research, in some cases, you are inviting failure and in other cases, you will be turning a blind eye to miracles and God's provision along the way. If you never knew there was a need, you certainly won't give God credit when he provides.

Measure twice, cut once

One of our biggest challenges early on in church planting was the learning curve on just how expensive it would be to rent space, even hourly space, in our prospective neighborhood. I called everyone, and I mean everyone that had prospective meeting spaces and came up empty. An up-and-coming area like ours was not very interested in renting to a church that didn't produce any tax revenue. Most places refused to even return my phone calls, emails, etc., but every failed connection was building my personal mainframe of information and teaching me the ins and outs of D.C. real estate. This was and still is a steep learning curve for someone called to minister and preach. Fortunately, every call was making me sharper and wiser. No's can be a real gift from God. The difference between something testing your patience and teaching you patience is simply a matter of perspective. Finally, one place I called was not a "no," but a "maybe."

The Courtyard Marriott Hotel in the Navy Yard was centrally located in the heart of our growth area. Not only that, but it was less than 100 yards from a metro stop. One afternoon, I was talking with David Godfrey and he asked about our progress on gathering prospective meeting space information. I told him the only real prospect was the Marriott Hotel. His ears perked up at the prospect. "Pursue that," he said hopefully. I called them back and asked how much they wanted, and my West Texas real estate ideals were obliterated. They wanted $1,100 per week for four hours on Sundays in their less than 2,000 square foot space. I was at a total loss. My buddy, Nolan, got a whole church, that's right, a whole huge church, for $1,000 a month! I'm talking offices, kid's space, a sanctuary, the whole package.

Granted, it was in Artesia, New Mexico , and not D.C., but still! My buddy, Tiny Diminguez did one better. God gave him an entire church and a parsonage to live in for free! All they had to do was remodel. When you ask Tiny how God blessed their church so greatly, his testimony always astounds. "You're not going to believe this, bro, but I just kept asking God to give us a church for free and he did."

What a great story! I wanted that to be my story, so I kept praying. However, instead of an older church, God sent a hardline offer from the Marriott of $1,100 per week and no one else. It seemed like an impossible amount of money. We didn't even have 10 people to come to the church on its first day yet. But, I remembered the words of my grandad: measure twice, cut once. So, before we committed the money to the Marriott, I called every single prospective rental property one more time just to make sure a new option had not come available. Just like cutting a piece of wood too short could cause it to be useless in a project, committing too much money to our space rental could leave us without money to reach people for the church. So, I called, and I prayed. Then I called and I prayed again. Finally, we took the leap! Faith and data are meant to coexist. The big equivalent of measuring twice and cutting once for a believer in Christ when pursuing a new creation can be summed up in this question: have you prayed about it? After taking in your information, and weighing your prospective plan, always allow God to offer input. You would be surprised the land mines you can avoid when trusting God with properly gathered research. He knows every twist and turn, especially before something new begins in his name.

His hands on mine

It is important to remember that God is the one guiding the formation of this glorious new creation, but he is using your hands to do it, just like my grandfather's hand on mine while using the saw. God's provision is unparalleled. His hands provide protection from harm while navigating foreign equipment. Your call to start something new will push you to look into things you never thought you would have need to understand. You will steward resources you feel inadequate to steward. The apostles can't believe that God would use them, as simple uneducated men, to be the vessels carrying the eternity altering gospel message. Wasn't there someone smarter, more capable or ... better? That's what I find myself saying to God when I feel like he is calling me to an impossible task. Isn't there someone better than me you could ask to do this? This attitude was not humility, but rather a misunderstanding of my role in the new creation.

You are not called to do this alone. God hands are on yours. He knows your gifts and your shortcomings. And, I've found through our new creation, that many times God's choice of you as his vessel has more to do with your shortcomings than your gifting. Let that sink in a minute. In our weakness, God is shown as strong. He is actually more visible when we clearly can't do something on our own. He never leaves us or forsakes us, especially in the midst of the impossible!

Next, his hands provide precision in crafting the new creation so that it is useful and accurate. You'll drive yourself mad thinking about every possible twist and turn your potential venture could take. We are called to do due diligence, but there will always be factors beyond our control. This is one of the first things a believer in Jesus Christ has to understand as they grow. Fear and worry are indicative of a faith problem. In the end, the way you sleep at night is directly connected to this question: Do I trust God? It really is that simple. Do you trust him with your situation? Your new creation? Your soul? His hands are on ours to navigate the finer points that only a true craftsman can handle.

Putting together a real strategy began to make people close to me nervous, especially my Dad. In the beginning, I found this to be odd because my Dad was a man of God, who had navigated his own new creations over the years, and he was the one who had taught me the principles of faith we just discussed in the previous section. So, over the course of the next few weeks, he started passing my name to churches in Texas that needed a pastor. Anytime someone refers you for a job it is a high compliment, especially your beloved father, but this seemed to have something behind it.

"I just don't see why you have to start something new when there are places out there, already, that you can help do better," Dad would say.

These words were heavy on my wife and me. My Dad was my hero and mentor, and I had a deep desire in my life for him to be proud of me, but I knew with every ounce of my soul that we were called to start Waterfront Church in Washington, D.C.! I had to please my Heavenly Father over desiring the approval of my earthly one. So, my wife and I began to pray for him. We begged the Lord for my Dad's blessing in our move to D.C. Notice I didn't say permission. Doing the Lord's will is between you and God alone. We prayed that the Lord would turn his heart to celebrate our venture with us and initially nothing happened except for more job offers. One particular job was high on Dad's list for us.

"Just hear them out," he said. "I've heard your Church plant idea, so hear out my idea. And don't mention D.C." So, I talked with their personnel team, not mentioning D.C. even once. It was a good talk.

Working on the new creation had made me sharper and full of vision. I left the call grateful for new friends, but still singular in our mission and focus to plant our church in D.C. The next day, my Dad called me. I was at home that afternoon, and when he called. I put it on speaker phone for my wife to hear too. I greeted him and asked if he had heard anything from the personnel team. His words shocked me. He said that he had been called by the chairmen of the team that morning, and that they wanted to go to the next step in offering me the job. But then, the chairman asked if there was something else that God was calling us to do, claiming that as they prayed about hiring us, the Spirit told them we had been "set aside for other things." Autumn and I couldn't believe it as we listened to Dad tell the story.

Finally, he broke. We could hear him crying through his next words. "Do you know why I've been against this?" he asked. "I have two reasons." We pastors always think in bullet points, it seems. "First, you're going to take my grandkids far away from Texas." At that time, we had two kiddos, Lulu (4) and Jack (2) and my wife would become pregnant soon after with our daughter, Harper! Lulu used to say her two best friends were Jesus and my Dad. She called him "Grandles," the perfect blend of grandad and our last name, Randles. Shout out to pastor Nolan Fredrick for coming up with that nickname. The two were inseparable until we moved. We knew this was hard for he and my mom out of love for our whole family. But, we had to go. Scripture says in Mark 10:29-30, "Truly I tell you," Jesus replied, "No one who has left home or brothers or sisters or mother or father or children or fields for me and the gospel will fail to receive a hundred times as much in this present age: homes, brothers, sisters, mothers, children and fields— along with persecutions—and in the age to come, eternal life." Ultimately, we are under Christ's authority, and the Lord knows that is hard to do with loving family involved. Your sacrifice is not forgotten!

We knew this was going to be a sticking point with Dad, but his second point caught us off guard. His tears increased dramatically. His voice was shaken as he spoke. "Second, I don't know how to teach you to plant a church." I still get emotional, even as I write this part of the story. Dad had done just about everything in ministry. He'd pastored for 20 years, been in itinerate evangelism for 20 years, worked for Fellowship of Christian Athletes, worked for the Baptist Convention, written and spoken for government agencies, done school assemblies, prison ministry, international ministry, athletic team chapels, college ministry, youth ministry ... everything under the sun you can do in ministry, except church planting. "You'll be going somewhere I can't guide you," he said. His fatherly heart was so evident. I was so proud to be his son that day. By this point, Autumn and I are crying too. "I have to do this," I tell him. "I know you do," he replied. "Know I'm on your team." Looking back, this was a critical moment for our new creation. We had resolved to follow God's leading above all else but prayed for his supernatural favor with my Dad and God had given it.

Strategizing had been the key to realizing how we were in need. The Lord knows what you need before you even ask him, but it a powerful thing when God's people put their needs into words. It is only then that we can fully appreciate the provision of God. After this, we began to speak about Waterfront Church with more confidence. It's amazing how a plan helps with that. Not long after that, Josiah and Natalie Gross, a young couple at the church in Lubbock said they were interested in coming with us to D.C. Natalie's family was living in Virginia, and Josiah was up for an adventure. He'd end up being our sound, video, and all-around media specialist for the church, and still is even to this day! Natalie was a talented musician and willing to serve as well. God had sent two of our finest volunteers and we didn't even know it! Having a plan helps people buy in and visualize what the person with the vision already sees. And then there were 7.

Chapter 9:
The Money's Gonna Come

In college, my favorite professors were the ones that gave you a review sheet before the midterm or final exams. I get that real life rarely hands you a review sheet, but it was still nice of them to do that for us. The review sheet lets you know how to prepare, and it typically lets you know what not to waste your time worrying about or committing to memory. Study sessions with a review sheet were simple, and virtually stress free, if you had been to class and had done the reading. They also produced a decent night's rest before the exam. Group study sessions consisted of going through the provided review, comparing notes, and then going to a movie or dinner afterward. But, without the precious review sheet, a much different experience awaits! Anything could be on the test! You scour the readings looking for insights, you reread your indecipherable class notes for clues, you desperately seek out contact info for that one friend you made in the class, hoping they took notes on the days you were absent, and then you sit alone at IHOP having them refill your coffee pot over and over while you cram every ounce of 'just in case' information into your strained, sleep-deprived and overloaded mind!

Okay, so maybe that was just me. Sometimes, without the comfort of a review sheet, I would find myself guessing on what the professor was going to deem important, and I would do my best to commit it to memory. Often times, it was not necessarily difficult to figure out what was important information for the exam, but every now and again, you'd run into a class with such a broad spectrum of material that it would be impossible to pinpoint an emphasis. So, you just made your decisions on what seemed important and then you prayed it was right. Have you ever studied the wrong things for a test before? That is a terrible feeling, especially if you really spent time trying to actually study.

One time in college, I was so concerned that a certain list was going to be on the final exam that I spent two weeks leading up to the final committing each word, each definition, and each concept to memory. I was waiting tables at Red Lobster at the time, and I had put my school notes in my waiter's book so that I could study in between tables when things got slow. I had been so worried about that list. It consumed me, and finally, on the day of the test, when the professor passed out the exams, I was shocked to find that less than ten percent of the final's points had been devoted to that list. All that time, there were WAY bigger things I should have been concerned with other than that list, but at the time, it was all I could think about. Yes, it was on the test, but it was only a piece of it, and a small one at that.

This leads me to the object of my most intense fears when it came to establishing a new creation: fundraising. Without money, our dream of planting a church in Washington, D.C., would never come to fruition. If we didn't have money, how would we live in the city? Where would the church meet for services? How could we advertise that we exist? How could anything work at all? Questions like this sat fundraising squarely on the throne in my mind as the monarch of my worry kingdom. And it wasn't just me — my wife had the same worry bug. One day during this stretch, she and I sat down separately and listed the pros and cons of planting a church in D.C. vs staying at a pre-existing church in Texas. It was bizarre. When we finished, we had extensive lists in each category except one. Under 'cons' for church planting in DC, we had both only written one 'con'. We had both written separately, "Steady Pay Check."

Wow. It was a God-inspired moment for us. Autumn looked at me and said, "If that's the only reason we would consider not doing this, then shame on us." She was right. Money always seems like a bigger problem than it really is. Just like the exam example, money can become the entire focus of your preparation, when it is really meant to be a fraction of the process. That being said, it is important to be diligent and professional in your pursuit of investors for your new creation.

This principle is doubly true for church planters and entrepreneurs. You are effectively asking people to put finances to something that exists in your mind or on paper. It is the reason that a launch plan, a brochure, a prayer card, a refrigerator magnet, architectural drawings, a picture of your target area, etc., are so important in the beginning. They are tangible things that represent the intangible vision you have received from God. It also shows people that you are serious about doing whatever you can to bring your vision to life.

A church planter without a launch plan is not ready for a significant financial investor. An entrepreneur without a business plan isn't either. Put together something tangible, professional, and inspirational that provides as accurate a picture as is possible of the vision God has given you. This is not 'fake it 'til you make it,' it's 'here's where we hope to go and here's how you can help.' The need for money brings out funny emotions in people. One group, like my wife and I, worries incessantly about it, giving it a priority it doesn't deserve. Another group seemingly pretends it's not even a real need. This is also faulty logic. Money is not the only thing to study, but it is also not meant to be underappreciated or underestimated.

God has all the money in the world at his disposal, but when he chooses to lavish it upon his servant in reaffirmation of a vision, it is meant to be celebrated and appreciated. This brings up the toughest part of fundraising: you have to be willing to ask people for money. I know this might seem obvious, but there are some of you reading this that HATE asking others for help, especially financially. Let me be clear: you cannot ever see God bring a new creation into existence without help from outside sources of faith. God's goal in giving a grand, glorious vision is that the world might see him clearly in the coming together of the miraculous. A vision for something new is never meant for you alone. God plans to use it to grow your faith and the faith of those around you.

A church planter that is afraid to ask people will not be a church planter for long. At the root of not wanting to ask people for money or help is the cancer of pride. Big pride makes for small faith. It also communicates to investors that are naturally curious about your product that you don't really believe the vision that has been given to you enough to go all in on it. Jesus said it best. "You do not have because you do not ask." Asking is an important part of the process. It enables the Holy Spirit to work in all kinds of ways. A conversation about money should always lead to a request for prayer from that individual, whether they commit to the project or not. I don't care how good a salesman you are; the conviction of the Holy Spirit can inspire an investor like no other!

We had people hear our sales pitch on the church plant in the most unlikely of meetings that would message back and tell us that after we asked their church or family for financial help that they felt the Holy Spirit leading for them to move to D.C. and help us get things started! When you can't ask for help, you have a pride problem. Plain and simple. Have the courage to ask. Our asking doesn't force God to bless us or force the hearer to give, but it does exhibit faith and courage when done with humility.

So, with a couple hundred dollars of our own money, Autumn and I put together a few hundred 5"x7" prayer cards with our family's picture on them along with a list of things to pray for and our contact information just in case they wanted to give. We made sure the picture included our two young children so that we looked extra needy. The card proclaimed our move to D.C. and our intent to start a church. I'm still so proud of that card. It took so much faith to actually put something in print.

We also called together our first ever Waterfront Church prayer meeting almost two years before we moved to D.C. so we could pass out the first round of cards to people we know would pray for us and hopefully seed the project so we could print our full launch plan and pay for the postage to send them out. One of our original board members, Kelli Lawrence, offered her home in Flower Mound, Texas, for the occasion, and she even catered it for free! This night would end up being pivotal in our understanding of fund-raising and the work of the Spirit. We had invited 40, what

I would consider, close ministry friends to the evening. I remember foolishly thinking all 40 of them would be there!

Autumn and I sat in the car together talking about how this evening was likely to play out. She asked me, "Will you ask them for money tonight?" I told her no. "We will let the cards do the asking for us." This was also foolish thinking. "How much do you think we will take in donations tonight?" she asked. I still can't believe I said this in response: "Somewhere between $20,000 and $30,000 for sure." Wow. Just, wow. The night unfolded a bit different than the script. When we walked in the house, we were greeted warmly by friends, but there weren't 40, there were 12. They were so kind to us, but initially there was more questions about if this was a response to me being unhappy in our current job than the call of God to take part in this new creation. I reassured them that we loved the church we were working for in Lubbock, but that this had always been the goal of our ministry.

That's when I passed out the cards and told the story of my vision. I watched them take in information as I talked. I watched them furrow their brows as they looked at the cards. I watched them try to see what God had placed in my heart. When I finished, they asked if they could pray for us. It was such a special time. They laid hands on Autumn and I and prayed for wisdom and favor for us. They prayed for our kids. They prayed for our marriage. They prayed for the new creation that they didn't fully understand, and Autumn and I cried with joy. It was like the journey became more real that night. That's what having the faith to ask for help will do. If it's just you, you can quit anytime with minimal issues, but once you've asked for help, there is an accountability that begins to develop.

The time seemed right. I finally got the guts to ask for financial partnership. The group kept smiling. I think I pictured thousand-dollar handshakes as we walked out the door. They didn't come. Not that night. Our friends hugged us, told us they would pray for us, and told us they were proud of us, but we did not receive one single check. Autumn and I got back into our car and stared at each other in disbelief. "We didn't get any money," she said. "It was such a great night, though!" She said exactly what I was thinking. The Spirit had moved that night, but we were no closer to having our startup capital.

About that time, we saw something on the windshield of our car. It was a piece of paper folded around a ten-dollar bill. I stepped out of the car, grabbed it, and got back in the car to read it with Autumn. The note read: "Take your wife to Starbucks on us! We are there for you!" Signed Michael and Kelli Tate. Oh, the irony! We came in expecting tens of thousands of dollars and left with ten bucks. But, irony would not be allowed to sully this great moment. It was Waterfront Church's first-ever donation! We had investors!

Not just financial investors, but prayer partners! We still have that ten-dollar bill! We learned another valuable lesson that day. Faith exhibited accumulates interest over time. The faith to get our friends together to share our vision and the courage to ask them to partner with us did not produce immediate financial dividends, but God used that room to help us greatly.

That room would end up giving us way more than the $20,000 to $30,000 we had initially hoped for, it would just take place over several years and not in one night. This is another great fundraising lesson. Very few people have the financial flexibility to immediately invest at full capacity. Their money is tied up other places, and they need time to figure out how they can partner with you. Don't see initial silence as rejection. Have follow-up conversations, and let the Spirit have time to work. One of the men there that night, John Crawford, called me a couple of months later and said that the Lord had told he and his wife, Tricia, to help us with several thousand dollars. He told a story about how his work situation was in jeopardy due to a downsizing in his company, but that God had told them to give to Waterfront Church anyway. Autumn and I both cried when we got the check. It was soaked in the faith of the Crawford family.

The church was never meant to be funded by thousand-dollar handshakes given flippantly by people with more money than they knew what to do with; it was meant to be a harbor of faith. We needed to respect the blessing God had sent and acknowledge the faith each gift was wrapped in. New creations are manifestations of faith. It takes faith to receive a vision. It takes faith to plan for that vision to become a reality, and it takes the faith of investors for the vision to become tangible. Until you can see that, and have a genuine gratitude for every cent invested, you will struggle raising funds.

And then there are times when you pray, you ask others for financial partnership, you are deeply grateful, you acknowledge faith, and you still don't get any initial investment ... from any one. Those are dark days. That's when calling becomes irreplaceable. Your new creation is something you are compelled toward by the Holy Spirit, and not just good thoughts or ideas. One day, for me, this particular concept came to a head. I had made the initial round of calls trying to raise our start-up capital and had come up but empty. A couple from Lubbock, Jeanie and Mike Chism (Jeanie is a dear friend and she would end up being one of our church's original board members) had given us just enough money to print our launch plans and pay for the postage to send them out. I still admire their faith to invest in a vision that was shaky at best at this point.

After the printing costs and the mailout, we were left with about $10,000 in our account from the Chisms, the

Crawfords, and the $10 from the Tates. Remember, we needed $1.3 million, but really closer to $2.5 million for our 5-year goal. We were just a few months from our projected move to D.C. and I got deeply discouraged. $1.3 million was all I could think of. It was in my dreams, my prayers, and just about every conversation, related or not. Remember, financial reasons were the only cons on our list for planting the church in the first place. There was a deep stronghold of fear that the Lord had to bust up before we could embark on this journey.

Jesus says, "Where your treasure is, there your heart will be also." I dearly treasured financial stability in my heart, and it was to become ingrained and more and more evident that the Lord desires for my heart to relocate closer to Him. During that time, I was booked to preach at a big student leadership camp in Texas called Super Summer. I was the preacher and dean for all the seventh-grade students that week. I loved Super Summer! It was a chance to share the gospel with and disciple students from all over the state, and because it took so many leaders to run, it was a chance to spend time with other likeminded student ministers, striving to live for Christ, blaze a trail for the kingdom of God. Every year, before the students arrived, we met for a time of consecration and prayer at the camp. Consecration is simply a time of prayer and worship to prepare your heart and mind for the work God has called you to. It is intense and highly important for anyone seeking to accurately reflect Christ in a heightened moment.

So, with friends and leaders experiencing an intimate time of worship all around me, I chose to spend my time worrying with God. "$1.3 million," I prayed. "$1.3 million." I said it over and over. To the onlooker, I probably looked like I was praying, but it was really the opposite. I could not get past this seemingly insurmountable need. How would God provide, and what would I do if He didn't? Finally, a real prayer came out on my thoughts. "Lord, please give me reaffirmation that this is going to happen." Now, just so you know, scripture says a wicked and adulterous generation asks for a sign, but to genuinely ask God for encouragement during a great faith exercise, is something different entirely. The attitude in approaching a need for a sign is that you will not comply with the Lord's wishes unless he jumps through your hoops. This is a faithless attitude and often warrants the Lord's rebuke rather than his favor.

In seeking reaffirmation, I was telling God that my spirit was aching from faith exertion, and that I needed encouragement to keep striving forward. Even Jesus is attended by angels in the Garden of Gethsemane as he stares death in the face. The key to reaffirmation from God is not making your participation in God's will contingent upon that reaffirmation. I believe one of the reasons Jesus calls the demand for a sign 'adulterous' is because you are flirting with the possibility of following your own will instead of your commitment to God's will. All this to say, from my worried but committed heart, I begged God for reaffirmation that my family would not starve, and that the church in D.C. would exist. What I'm about to tell you is miraculous. Many times, God's reaffirmation happens over time rather than in a lightning bolt, but this was an exception.

A mere seconds after praying this prayer, with the worship band playing on stage and youth ministers praying all around me, a young pastor from West Texas made his way toward me. He put his hand on my shoulder, leaned into my ear and said, "I don't know what this means, but God told me to tell you the money's gonna come." I immediately begin to cry. God, in his infinite kindness, had seen fit to send a messenger to ease my weary heart. I told the man thank you and just how important his words had been. It was just what I needed. As he walked off, another man was headed my way. This guy was from the other side of the state in East Texas. He also put his hand on my shoulder and uttered the same words. "Bro, I don't even know what this means but the Holy Spirit told me to tell you the money's gonna come." Now I'm really crying. Twice. God had reaffirmed his vision for our church twice in a matter of minutes, moments after I had asked for reaffirmation. Now, I really had no choice but to trust. With these miracles and those we had already experienced, there was no way God had not destined our church to exist! God had just given us a promise: the money's gonna come. And it did. Above and beyond what we could have asked for or imagined. The week we moved, the account had more than $200,000 in it! That was plenty with 12 baskets full left over to give us confidence in reaching our community!

Fundraising also has one more major impact on your new creation; as you present your vision, it provides an on ramp for others to catch the vision and join your team. There was scarcely a fundraising event for Waterfront Church that I spoke at that a person or family didn't come up afterward and ask us to pray for them because they were thinking of moving their family to D.C. with us! The first time this happened was during our very first ever fundraiser. It took place at First Baptist Church in Plains, Texas, and was led by my buddy, Patrick Hamilton. He let me preach Sunday morning to his congregation in the heart of cotton country, and I brought our worship leader with me. He was going to give me an opportunity to present the vision of Waterfront Church to his people that night. After the meeting at Kelli and Mike's house, I had learned to temper fundraising expectations, but we were very hopeful that night.

First Baptist Church of Plains and its members would end up funding a huge portion of the project. Never, ever judge a book by its cover when it comes to fundraising. First Baptist Church of Plains was not the biggest church we presented to, but they would end up being one of the most generous and kind.

At the end of the presentation, a couple made their way over to me, asking a ton of questions. Both worked in education, their kids were grown, and they were praying for an adventure. That's how we met the church's original hostess, Stephanie Brock, and her husband, Coach Craig Brock. Coach would end up doing every odd job in the book for us. He was our first usher, a pillar on the set-up crew, a fill in trailer driver (when the church was portable), and a source of great encouragement to my family and the new families in the church. They had such great faith that they dipped into their retirement to help fund their living expenses in D.C. It is important to remember that when you ask for investors, that you need much more than money to get started. Having the faith to ask enables God to fulfill every need, even the ones you don't see yet. No new creation has a chance if you don't find the courage to ask for help. And then there were 9. Suddenly, the room wasn't seeming so empty.

Chapter 10:
Deploying is Complicated

Have you ever gotten territorial with someone because you felt ownership over something? My wife and I love taking our young kids to the park, and from time to time they decide that a piece of playground equipment belongs to them, whether they are using it or not. Our beautiful daughter Harper does this most often with the teeter totter. This is particularly funny because it is an item that requires two people in order to enjoy it. She just wants to possess it. As soon as we get to the park, she runs to the playground, finds the teeter totter and begins to play keep away. Like a burglar alarm, she shrieks anytime someone comes within a certain proximity of the item. After a few minutes of this show, we eventually decide to parent her, and we begin the process of leading her away from the teeter totter so that other kids can enjoy it.

This is easier said than done, but eventually she finds something or someone else to play with. She does not own the public playground; the taxpayers do. She does not possess the teeter totter; it is meant to be shared, but you would never know that by her attitude. When God calls you to a new creation, He often leads you to a place that the devil has felt ownership over. This feeling of ownership could not be further from the truth. The earth is the Lord's and everything in it. The devil has no more ownership of the things of this world than our daughter did over the teeter totter on the public playground. However, our daughter's actions at the playground could lead you to think she had power over it.

That, my friends is the role of the devil when God calls you to step out in faith to inspire a new creation. He is a powerless toddler seeking to trick you into thinking that things belong to him that actually belong to God. He will shriek at the top of his lungs in hopes of scaring you or annoying you out of the picture, but the Lord intends to lead him away in defeat. John writes, "Greater is he that is in me than any power that's in this world." That means that if we have Jesus, then we win! The Bible also says, "Resist the devil and he will flee from you." He has the ability to distract and discourage you but can be squashed in his tracks in the name of Jesus and a little resistance.

That being said, the loudest shrieks from the devil in an attempt to thwart God's plan of establishing His new creation, came in the months leading up to our first service. During that stretch, so many major changes would take place in every aspect of my life, that when I look back at pictures and videos from that time I hardly recognize the young man I was, compared to who I've become. I have come to understand that conflict and growth seem to go hand and hand. God provides peace in the storm, but we cannot shy away from the prospect of turmoil if we intend to grow. So, we set a moving day for our family on the calendar, (January 2014) as well as a day to start services in D.C. (Easter 2014). It was around that time that the stable ground beneath us began to shift. The pastor I had been working for in Lubbock, Brad Jurkovich had just announced that he would be leaving our church to take a job pastoring in Bossier City, LA. Brad is a dear friend and an original part of our Waterfront Church board, but his departure was troubling because he had committed the Lubbock church to be our primary church partner (in the church-planting world, we call this our sending church) and we were uncertain as to if his move would jeopardize that partnership.

To this point, Victory Life Church in Lubbock had committed $10,000 per year for 5 years to help us get started, along with help doing our books, etc., but now things were unsure. You never know when a strategically placed change from God will turn a fearful moment into a multiplied blessing. Pastor Brad going to Bossier City would immediately produce another influential partner that is still blessing our journey all these years later, but at the time, all I could feel was fear. To make matters more complicated, according to the bylaws for Victory, I, as the associate pastor, would become the interim pastor of the church, assuming weekly preaching responsibilities, and would become the head of the pastor search committee. This was a church of around 1,000 so it was no small task, all the while still preparing to launch Waterfront Church in a few short months. Lots of days were spent working 7 a.m. to 5 p.m. on Victory Life stuff, and then 6 p.m. to 11 p.m. on Waterfront fundraising.

From the very beginning, our will and our commitment to the vision God had given was tested. A few days after Brad resigned, I met with the Victory leadership team for what would be our first pastor search committee meeting. I can still remember Robert Madden, another dear friend and faithful Waterfront Church supporter, looking at me and saying, "I think we already have our man." It was the highest level of flattery for me. The thought of getting to stay at the church I loved (Victory was a miracle in its own right) and had been serving in for four years, in the town I loved, with people we loved, while making a steady paycheck was quite an offer. But, we had to see the vision through. How could we not? Too much had happened to reaffirm our path to D.C. for us to cut and run now. The vision gave us faith and the Holy Spirit gave us the resolve to decline without wasting a moment on consideration. As a side note, whenever God has called you to something fresh and fragile like our new creation, it is sinful to even consider other options. It is an emotional affair seeking to divide your allegiance and intimacy with God and a plot of the enemy to distract you from the task at hand.

I wanted to consider his offer, which at this point still needed the affirmation of the rest of the group, but all I could think of was the story of Lot's wife turning into a pillar of salt when she followed God's leading away from her home, but longingly looked back one last time in sin. I also thought of Jesus' words in Luke 9: "No one who puts their hand to the plow and looks back is fit for service in the kingdom of heaven." Crooked fields produce a weak harvest. So, I smiled a broken smile at Robert, thanked him for the affirmation and then said, "I think you guys can do a whole lot better than me." This was a massive moment in our journey to start Waterfront Church. We had sacrificed a chance at the comforts of home to pursue the vision. It has been my experience that God honors sacrifice in whatever form we present it.

That meeting was also the first time I got to see just how complicated Victory's circumstances were. Money in churches typically gets tight when a pastor moves away, but when that pastor has been with the church since the beginning, I have found this principle to be especially true. The church needed some personnel, facility, and budgetary moves that were beyond my level of leadership and expertise at the time and we needed to look for help.

"Would your Dad help us?" asked Scott Hicks, another Victory Leadership team member. Scott would also become the most indispensable member of our Waterfront Church board in the first few years. It was quite an idea. My Dad was beyond qualified to help us with an interim. He had served as a head pastor for almost 20 years and had been traveling as an evangelist for 20 more after that. He had preached at our church numerous times and was a source of wisdom for me, the former pastor and members of the Victory Leadership team—but would he come off the road to take the job? Dad had been offered pastorates numerous times throughout his years in evangelism. Really good jobs, too. And it's not that Victory wasn't a good job—Dad had just been in pretty high demand, especially in his hometown of Lubbock. I told them I would ask about Dad becoming our interim, but I was less than optimistic. Little did I know that the Holy Spirit was hard at work on my mom and Dad, preparing them for a massive change.

Chapter 11:
Durable Vision

D ad loved to preach, and I mean it when I say he was the best I've ever listened to. The Lord used him to build churches, navigate impossible circumstances, and to take the Gospel message all over the world. Because his leadership arsenal was so versatile, he was like a one-stop shop for any problem that you had. He'd seen it all and he was gifted to articulate in a way you could understand about how to get out of or thrive in whatever your complex situation was. For this reason, Dad got a lot of offers to come off the road to pastor, but he would never take one because he loved doing what he was doing.

So, the day I called him about the Victory job, I thought he would say no and instead offer names for who would be good for us. He was well versed in all things Victory Life because he had served as a confidant for me and also for Pastor Brad in the past. He was also well versed in all things to do with the city of Lubbock because he and my mom had grown up there and lived there for decades. Dad was strangely quiet on the call. I thought at any moment he would chime in with a name or two to help us. Finally,

I just asked to him, "Do you want the job?" His response was one word. "Maybe."

I was shocked. He'd be perfect for the job, and he would also be the ultimate defender of our new creation. I was beyond excited. I set up a meeting the very next week with the search team to introduce Dad (again) to them. They were sold, and I could see Dad was too. After the meeting, we got back into his black Dodge Ram pickup truck, and Dad made an unexpected request.

"If I do this, I need you to stay a little longer." His words initially made me furious. "Dad, we can't stay—we have to go," I said with more defiance than conviction. His next words were true wisdom. "I need you to help through the transition. I need you to make the handoff to me." It was the first of October and we were three months from our D.C. move date. It felt like the vision was slipping away. Or, that this was a test. Or, that my Dad was making one last play to keep the grandkids close. "How long?" I asked sheepishly. "Give me 6 months," Dad replied.

This was a tall order at this point. This would bump our move to the end of April, and it would bump our church services to a fall launch instead of an Easter launch. In the span of a few brief moments, I felt my frustration melt into peace. It was supernatural. Sometimes the Lord uses our flexible spirit to provide some of his richest blessings. I agreed.

We'd stay six months and help make the handoff. I had no idea what our obedience would produce for Waterfront Church, my family or for me. A chance to obey the Lord rolls in like a wave to the shore. Just like the waves keep coming, there are countless opportunities to obey, and a true disciple seeks to constantly say yes to even the smallest of things. Dad was genuinely grateful. He called a meeting of the elders and laid out the new plan, but he changed a few things in relation to me and Victory's commitment to Waterfront Church.

He started by telling me I was getting a raise in pay for my last six months at Victory. A BIG raise. I couldn't believe it. Part of me thought this was a ploy to keep us in Texas, but then he followed with something even more amazing. He told the elders that victory's commitment of $10,000 per year for the first five years of our church plant was a decent investment in a church plant, but it was not nearly enough of a gesture for a church claiming to be the primary sending partner when the East Coast was so expensive. "I think $25,000 a year indefinitely sounds about right." My jaw hit the floor. I watched the elders not only agree on the decision but celebrate it as well. I cried. The last blessing that came from staying in Lubbock for six extra months was hidden at this moment. These are blessings shrouded in God's sovereignty—things we cannot know are vitally important, but the author of all space and time is keenly aware of what's happening.

As you know from earlier chapters, my Dad is my hero. The greatest gift God had given me by staying in Lubbock through that stretch is that I got to work side by side as Dad's right-hand man for six very special months. At the time, I remember feeling like we were best friends. We both loved to work. He had more ministry knowledge than anyone I knew, and I had extensive knowledge of the people in the church from five years serving there. I remember He constantly wanted to teach me life and ministry lessons through that stretch. Several mornings before 7 a.m. he would just show up at our house in his cowboy hat because he wanted to spend time with our kids.

He would talk about when he got too old to preach that he would love to be my limo driver taking me places to preach all across the country. Never in my life have I desired a limo or a driver, but for some reason, it sounded cool from him.

"We're partners," he would say. I felt it. By staying just a few extra months, I got something I had always dreamed about—I got to be my Dad's best friend. Living with him as a kid was great but working with him to further the Kingdom of God was a piece of heaven.

A vision from God is not fragile like a ceramic figurine. It is durable and able to stand the test of time and the elements because God is the one who has willed it into being. Our God doesn't build fragile things. His creations last. In some cases, they are eternal. Carry confidence in knowing that if the spirit of God changes the plan, that it was for the good! Those months flew by, but I can remember just about every individual day with my Dad. It would end up being my only chance at them.

Chapter 12:
Never Simple

As our week to move approached, we were filled with anticipation. Prayer times were becoming more intense, our plan of action was coming into focus, and the money was coming in. It was actually happening! Our new creation was taking shape. All we had left to do was pack up the house, load the moving truck, and attend our commissioning service the following Sunday. It would not be that simple. Things were at work that only Almighty God could know. Please know you are not reading the thoughts of a cynic. Sometimes God lays out a plan, and it really is that simple. This was not one of those.

On the Tuesday before moving, I had gone into work as usual and about 10 a.m. got a call from Autumn saying that Jack, our 2-year-old at the time, had been huffing and puffing with very irregular breathing. We took him to the hospital for what would later be diagnosed as a respiratory virus producing respiratory distress. Jack was breathing so fast it was causing his little heart to almost beat out of his chest. He was taken immediately to the pediatric ICU, and the doctors were discussing putting him in a coma just to slow him down. We were shocked. This had come out of nowhere, and we were scared. Jack's first two days in the ICU were very scary, and we found ourselves wondering if our move would be halted again. That Thursday, Autumn and I left the hospital in shifts to sign the papers on the sale of our house not knowing how this would play out. Every step of the way we prayed.

There are certain stretches in life that require consistent petition of God on how to proceed. He is the great encourager, the great creator and, especially in Jack's case, the great physician. God carried us every step of the way. That same Thursday, with almost no notice, Dad rallied about 25 people from the church to load the moving truck for us so we could stay with Jack in the ICU. We couldn't believe it. Several people even cleaned our house so we could be out on time. It was a team effort. Oh, and did I mention that our daughter was only 2 months old at the time?! Several people helped with babysitting and others lavished blessings on our other daughter Lulu in the form of toys and play dates while we were at the hospital.

On Friday, Jack was finally released from the hospital. His sudden illness had put multiple things into perspective. First, we realized that our family was fair game for attacks from the enemy. There was a spiritual element to Jack's struggle, and I believe that planting our church invited that. Second, there was a realization that countless factors are completely beyond our control. During these times, prayer is your finest weapon to defend your hope. We prayed a lot that week. Because all of our furniture and clothing was on the moving truck, we spent Friday through Sunday night with my parents. It was meant to be a time of celebration before the sadness of saying goodbye, and all that Jack had been through had us looking to breathe easy for a couple of days.

What would happen next was nowhere on our radar. Not in a million years. Autumn and the kids were booked to fly out Monday morning, and my Dad and I had planned to make the 26hour cross-country drive from Texas to D.C. with our family car. It was a dream of mine to make that trip with him. He loves history so much, I couldn't wait to hear all of his brilliantly boring tidbits of information, like our family vacations of old. But even that plan would come to a screeching halt.

Saturday night at my parent's house was a pivotal night. Dad, who had been so strong throughout our rough week with Jack, was hurting. I still vividly remember him lying in bed and gripping his stomach that had swollen up like a balloon. Dad had never had a major illness before, so the thought of it being something serious was the furthest thing from our minds. My sister and I stood by his bed that night cracking jokes about his appendix rupturing because we never actually thought his situation could be anything worse than that. Hayley would read the Wikipedia description of the symptoms of appendicitis, like pain in the abdomen, and she would then make the symptom true by playfully pinching Dad hard in the stomach. Dad would cry out in half fake and half real pain, totally playing along.

About 11 p.m. on Saturday night, Dad asked me if I would preach the next morning at my own commissioning service because he hurt too bad not to go to the hospital. Dad never turned down a chance to preach, let alone find a way out of it. I genuinely thought this was highly irregular but still nothing to be too concerned about. Dad headed to the hospital, and I stayed up all night writing my sermon. I always loved preaching at Victory, and Dad and I were like a one-two punch. He was the one who taught me to preach after all! The morning services were great, the commissioning was powerful, and I drove Autumn and the kids to the hospital afterwards to see what I thought would be my same old Dad, just less his appendix.

When we got to the hospital room it was still a lot of laughs, but a new mystery emerged. Dad said, "It's not my appendix, it's my pancreas." At this point, to all of us, Dad included, pancreas was just another word. And pancreatitis just seemed like something that would be easily treatable. We had no idea what this pain in Dad's abdomen really meant or how serious it was. God was so good to keep us in the dark. If he hadn't, I'm not sure we would have left for D.C. that day. Or ever.

Sometimes, God is kind to let plans change slowly, even though he knows the end result and could unfold the plans quickly. In his infinite kindness, he places the things we fear into our blind spots, so that even though they are present, they are not a factor in our decision making. So, that was it for our triumphant exit from Lubbock. We hugged Dad, prayed for him, the kids kissed him goodbye and we walked to the car parked at the Covenant Hospital in Lubbock, Texas not realizing that a particularly wicked cancer was ravaging Dad's organs.

When we got to the parking lot, I told Autumn I'd take her and the kids to the airport and prepare to drive it alone since Dad was out. "I don't think so," she replied. "We stay together." It was the perfect statement to end this portion of our story. Please know the heaviness from her end of what she had just said—'we stay together' meant 26 hours on the road rather than 3 hours in the air accompanied by my mom, with a 4-year-old, a 2-year-old, and a 2-month-old.

It was the right decision. We needed each other. It is a wicked thing to love God less than the people and things he's created, but it is also wicked to forget that God gave us each other because it is not good for us to be alone. So, like the pioneers of old, headed West to seek their fortune, my family, as well as our worship leader and his wife, loaded the wagons and headed East. With our families, we added to our core group. And then, there were 13.

Chapter 13:
God Sends Help

Pulling into D.C. was a surreal experience. If you've ever planned something for more than a decade you know what I'm talking about. That day was one that I had played countless times in my head, running countless scenarios of what it would be like and what I would be saying. It was an unbelievably heavy experience.

I strongly believe that the devil hates new creations with a special vigor. They seek to reclaim things, people and places that the devil falsely thinks have belonged to him. The devil knows he cannot thwart the ways or plans of God, but he can certainly attempt to mess with the visionary to confuse wisdom, exasperate fears, and whisper doubt. It is the reason that the devil refuses to do battle with almighty God—he knows he will lose every time. However, we are a different story. The devil chooses to do battle with believers because, even though our God is stronger, our belief in our own strength makes us susceptible to a prideful fall.

On this particular trip, the devil's attack came in the form of a heaviness that weighed on me from the moment we pulled into the city. I couldn't believe we'd actually done it. We had moved from Texas to the East coast. We had left our friends. We had left my Dad in the hospital. And the church was legitimately nonexistent. I remember telling Autumn that first week that I did not have time to unpack boxes because I needed to go to work. Where exactly was work? We had no building. I had no office. There was no congregation at this point. I just knew I need to be working.

That's one thing about me and my character—I genuinely love to work. For better or worse. Hear me say this: my work ethic did not build Waterfront Church. The church grows because God wants it to grow. His will is paramount. However, in addition, I believe God has called us to serve with all our hearts, realizing that there are eternal implications to our efforts. I cannot think of a single example of a new creation pioneer that wasn't a self-starter. When you are a part of something new, there is no one telling you where to go and what to do aside from the vision God has given you itself. You must be willing to strategize, work hard from start to finish each day, and then get up the next morning and do it all over again. All the while, you believe you are working toward something that at any point, might not actually come to exist.

Remember God's promises, saturate your mind with scripture and press on! I still remember my first real day at work. I went to the neighborhood Starbucks in the Department of Transportation Building that faces M Street SE. I found a spot by the window, and I began writing thank-you notes to people who had invested in our endeavor. If I'm being honest, I was very scared at this point. I've found in my walk with God that fear can be easily combatted with gratitude. In this case, remembering that I wasn't alone and that we had partners praying for us and lifting us up was huge. So, my job at Waterfront began with thank-you notes. I also started scheduling meetings with area pastors to see how we could partner with them and if they would partner financially with us.

One of those meetings, that very first week, was with a pastor in Spotsylvania, VA. He was gracious enough to come up to D.C., and I started driving him around our neighborhood giving him the tour and trying to show him we were in need. We stopped the car in SW D.C. in front of a church covered with graffiti. It was my 'close the deal' spot. The church was the first church built by freed slaves in the district, and it now sat covered in graffiti, by a professional, that seemed to want it to look like anything but a church. It was the best-selling spot for our vision because it was a picture of how our neighborhood felt about religion in general. If it wouldn't go away, could it at least not remind people of a church at all?

I was in the process of explaining the vision in the car when all of the sudden a huge group of college students walked past the car. I felt the Holy Spirit kick that I needed to pay attention even though I was talking to this man, hoping to win his church's support. I noticed that the students, about 20 of them, had their lips moving, but they were not talking to each other. All the sudden, it hit me like a ton of bricks. They were prayer walking! They were walking through our neighborhood and asking for God to give them direction. I could feel it. So, I very abruptly halted my sales pitch, right at the good part, and I excused myself from the car and walked toward the college kids. "Hey guys," I called, "Are you guys prayer walking?" At this, their blank faces erupted in excitement. "Yeeesss!!!!!" They excitedly came towards me. Their smiles were ear to ear, and I was just at a loss for words at how encouraging they were.

Their leader was a college student named Alexis, and they had come to D.C. on a mission trip from Southeastern University in Florida. Alexis said that the church they had come to help had not actually needed anything on this particular day and the group has been praying for someone with a like-minded mission to help. I told her that we had just moved to D.C. to start a church and that we could use some help unpacking and washing clothes. The students were so gracious. It was just so Waterfront. God had sent us our first mission team, and we didn't even know them before their first day on the job. Autumn was beautifully overwhelmed by their kindness too. They had been sent by

God himself to care for our church even when our church was just a couple of pastoral families.

Just for the record, I didn't have to sell that pastor on our church after that. He was in! The Lord had closed the deal with a miracle. A similar thing happened the day we moved into our apartment. God provided Texas friends, Norman Flowers and Loyall Watkins from Oak Street Baptist Church in Graham, TX, another church partner, to be in D.C. without us knowing it, and they showed up and built our beds and helped unload the moving truck! Timing belongs to the Lord. All resources are at his disposal. His reach knows no limits. And his love for his missionaries is extravagant.

Chapter 14:
I Don't Know How to Do This

After a week of settling into our 11th floor apartment on I street SE with the help from our new friends from Florida, it was time to get to work. But, where should we begin? There is a truly overwhelming feeling that comes with figuring out where to lay your first foundation stones. Writing thank-you notes was preparation work for the future as well as me staying on top of fundraising, but we had moved to D.C. to plant a church. That was the vision, not just to live in a cool place. My Dad powerfully told me that week, in between his medical tests, that I had mastered the art of fundraising and that now I needed to switch gears to doing the work of church planting. At first, I told him he was being silly. Of course, we had moved here to plant a church. His reply was important. "Sometimes we put off things we don't know how to do in favor of things we already know how to do because it requires less faith." Deep wisdom.

In the beginning especially, a new creation requires you to try a whole collection of new leadership muscles. You also have fewer day-to-day accountability from your supervisors, if you have any at all, and the person tasked with keeping you on target is yourself. The freedom for creativity is unparalleled, but the potential for wasted time and holes in your plan are greatly increased as well.

Work hard every day.

This is a critical truth, but it is only half of your daily responsibility. You should also work smart every day so, are you doing right by your new creation by doing what needs to be done? There is a type of person that pursues a new creation for the simple goals of having a more flexible schedule without being forced to do work they don't want to do. If that describes you, let me just say there are a lot easier ways to get what you're looking for than to pursue a new creation, as a church planter, an entrepreneur, an inventor, or founder. Flexibility and responsibility are married. You are only as flexible as your responsibilities will allow.

God has positioned you as the point of leadership for his work. The vision for something new does not exist for your pleasure. God may greatly bless you in the process, but the goal is to submit yourself to God by receiving and shepherding that to which you were called. You are a steward of talents, just like Jesus' parable, put them to work and produce a profit! Those who bury the talent to have a more flexible schedule and remain free from doing things they don't like to do will not get to have a long-term place in the world of the new and what work they have done will benefit someone else's new creation.

I had to pull back from the comfort of fundraising (if you can believe that) to start building our church. This really was a change in mindset. A constant problem for any growing church is figuring out how to really love and lead all the people that God sends you. We have a rule amongst our church staff that we are to avoid favoritism, but that we would strive to treat everyone God sends us equally WELL. The key word is of course "well." No matter what your line of work is—ministry, sales, management, etc.— you realize early on that treating everyone equally with a glowing result is not possible. Some people require more time, and some have issues that are more complicated. Some people need encouragement and others need counsel. Some people need food to eat and others immediately need the message of Jesus.

Once we learn who people are and what they need, we know how to proceed in loving them, caring for them and, in some cases, learning from them. We must see each person as an equally loved creation of the Living God, but we must see their giftings, short-comings and situations as clues for how we should interact with them to best push them towards Christ. The Son of God illustrated this principle to perfection for us when he performed miracles. Sometimes, he simply speaks, and the person is healed. Sometimes, he touches the person and they are healed. One time, he actually spit on the dirt and rubbed the mud on a man's eyes to bring back his sight. In each case, it was exactly what was needed to bring peace to the person's body and their soul as well.

He loved them equally, but he cared for them in different ways. It is a powerful thing to really get to know someone. This principle is also true when you are getting to know Jesus. As a disciple striving to grow and deepen in your relationship with him, moments will come up where you realize a new extent of God's awesome power, and it will change how you live your life forever. Realizing who God truly is changes everything.

All this to say, a week into our tenure in D.C., I called our only lead, Brad Morris. You may remember Brad from an earlier chapter. He was a high school student on our very first mission trip to D.C. and he had since grown up and had gone to work as a staffer on the hill for a congressman from Oklahoma. Just the thought of Brad still makes me smile. As long as I've known him, he's always been a joy filled Christ follower and encourager. He was the perfect first meeting. I can't begin to tell you how nervous I was to call him. Remember, we didn't really know anyone else, so a friendly encounter was becoming saturated in pressure.

I called Brad and asked him if I could meet with him, hoping to sell him on being the first D.C. member of our church. Brad was very kind and then upped the ante. "Why don't you come to my office, and I'll introduce you around." Brad didn't know it at the time, but his request terrified me. He didn't have just any office. He worked at the Capitol, and I had never been inside the Capitol before. In the midst of all our mission trips to D.C., I had never actually gone through one of the most famous tourist spots in the world. The Capitol dome is literally at the center of the District of Columbia and can be seen all over the city.

I couldn't say no, but I also felt ill equipped. Brad picked a time, not too far off and I did my best to prepare. As the day approached, I was too afraid to ask Brad for a dress code—I didn't want to sound dumb—so my wife and I went back and forth on whether I should be myself or wear my suit. Anyone who knows me knows I rarely ever wear suits. I'm pretty much a wedding and funeral only suit wearer. Part of that is due to my ever-expanding waistline, but part of it is because I always felt that in the context of our personal ministry, I needed to look accessible to all the different people we interact with. There is such a massive gap between the haves and have nots in D.C., and I wanted to bridge the gap between them, even in the way I dressed, if it meant they might hear more clearly the gospel message I was sharing. To this day, it's the reason, I preach to congressional officials, ambassadors, government employees, restaurant employees, and the homeless in jeans every Sunday.

In a city that is buttoned up during the work week it has been special to see diversity thrive under the message of Christ paired with low barriers to entry. The lost don't know how to act saved. They just know something is missing, and we know what they are missing is Jesus! Sadly, fear won out on this day and instead of being myself, I put on a three-piece suit I'd had for about a decade. The suit really symbolized my mindset that day. It was too tight and made me feel uncomfortable. It was older in style and not cool. I also felt this way. Most urban churches I'd studied had really hip pastors with great style and physique. That has not ever been me. The suit was also disingenuous. No one knew us in the city, but Brad and I was starting off our mission trying to be what I thought I should be and not who God had called me to be.

It was with this cloud that I walked the mile from our apartment up New Jersey Ave toward the Capitol. Autumn was nervous for me too. I remember looking up at our 11th floor apartment window from the street and seeing a figure waiving at me as I walked. I've got the best wife in the world. She would later say she was crying in the window because she knew a lot of my confidence was tied up in this meeting. I did one thing right leading up to that meeting. I brought my bible. I treat my bible like a security blanket quite often.

That's why God gave it! It is a tangible reminder that God is with you. Pressing the scriptures to my chest like a child would a teddy bear, I walked in the Capitol and made my way to Brad's office.

When I walked in, he greeted me immediately. He was in jeans and a flannel shirt! I'll never forget he hugged me, and grinning ear to ear he said, "Why are you in a suit? It's recess!" I had no clue what recess was other than the recess school children experience on the playground. Brad explained, "Our member is out of town, so we can be a bit less formal this week. I thought if I invited you during recess, you'd feel more comfortable." Sigh. Brad took me around his office and introduced me to his co-workers and friends. Brad told stories of when I was his student minister and really bridged the gap for me. He was a true godsend. I've told Brad this many years later, but while he was introducing me around, I was praying feverishly in my head. I was asking God how I could possibly do what he had called me to do in planting Waterfront Church. I was telling him that I didn't even know what recess was, let alone how to lead people leading a nation. I even came just short of telling God I wanted to go home. It erupted in this simple prayer—"Lord, I don't know how to do this!"

Let me be clear—these are lies from the enemy. To say you are inadequate is a half- truth. We are inadequate for the matters of eternity, but as an instrument in the hand of almighty God, commissioned by him to do his work, we cannot fail. The devil's scheme is as old as time. He tries to remind you who you are on your own so that you will fearfully fold. In turn, God reminds us that we are not alone in Christ Jesus, and he will uphold us with his righteous right hand. About this time, Brad asked if I wanted to tour the floor of the House of Representatives. I said sure and off we went. We rode this 'secret' underground Capitol train, which was awesome by the way, and we walked past security and onto the floor. It was beautiful. I couldn't believe it. After walking around and looking at everything my eyes could take in, Brad asked me to have a seat in one of the member chairs.

We stared at the seat where the speaker of the house sits and then Brad asked a question that would change my mindset about D.C. forever. "So, I've been studying the book of Jeremiah and there are some things I don't understand. Can you help me?" God used this question to transform my mind. Up until this point, I had been questioning why God had chosen me for this task when I felt so inadequate. But in one question, I realized that God had not sent me to teach politicians how to govern or staffers how to officiate the office, he had not sent me to bring insight into state or city affairs. I didn't know how to do those things, but I did know scripture! The answer to Brad's question rested firmly in my grip, even while sitting in this seat of power. I knew scripture. And God had sent me to teach the people of D.C.

to hear the voice of the Holy Spirit. I could see my purpose, and I knew my role.

This is a huge moment for any entrepreneur. When doubt and fear seek to destroy you, remember who you are and what exactly God made you to do. You cannot be the savior of the world. Only Jesus could be that. And so, I'm proud to say that the very first Waterfront Church bible study took place on the floor of the House of Representatives in the book of Jeremiah when I least expected it. Later that day, I walked down the hill with my head high, my sleeves rolled up and my jacket over my shoulder. The Lord has always been in control, but now I believed it, and that is a powerful place for a disciple to be. Brad would introduce us to Riley Pagett and his wife, Lauren, along with a young man named Adam Ferris. Both Adam and Riley would become two of our first deacons. And then there were 16.

Chapter 15:
First Outing

Have you ever watched a movie based around a well-known, historic event? The writers have built the entire script around a countdown to what the audience already knows is going to happen, but the characters in the movie are still in the dark. The easiest example of this is James Cameron's 'Titanic.' The audience watches the forbidden love affair between Leonardo DiCaprio and Kate Winslet while thinking to themselves, 'if only they knew what was ahead!' It is that tension that drives the story. This doesn't just happen with tragedies. It is also the premise of most romantic comedies. You know the couple ends up together, but the movie shows us how the relationship began and the obstacles they overcame to live happily ever after. Art imitates life in this line of thinking. Movies with this kind of tension are compelling to watch, but when it is real life–YOUR life–it forces a realization that God is the one directing our steps and writing our story.

Waterfront Church was still 2 and a half months from our first service, and we had no idea apart from the vision God had given us that the church would even get off the ground. There was an epic battle taking place between fear and faith in my heart and my wife's heart. When you move your family half way across the country away from family and your support system to start something that only exists in a vision, you know this battle is coming. Not knowing if anyone would come, we invited every person we could think of to our church's very first outing: A Washington Nationals baseball game! Our church has a very intimate relationship with the game of baseball. Our church's first services (and every service since, for the record) have taken place less than 100 yards from the closest metro stop to the Washington Nationals Ball Park. So, when we were planning the first ever church outing in the summer before our launch, we, of course, knew that the ballpark had to be involved.

The stadium is only a couple of blocks from where our church would be meeting, and it just made sense. We even bought all the tickets so that it would be free. The event was draped in hidden faith because we didn't have the money or really even the confirmed people to attend that would assure this event was a success. The greatness of God had been disguised in this moment as He laid the foundation for our church.

Most of those in attendance with us at the game you've already heard about, but there were other founding leaders there that night too. One of the potential church prospects there was Kylie Mills. We had met Kylie briefly while in Lubbock but had no idea she would end up such a key piece in our church's story. She was the first person to receive Christ at Waterfront Church and she was our second baptism. She also would end up bringing lots of people to the church. She was a gift from God to Autumn as well. She often referred to Kylie as her first friend in D.C. After the game was over, she had her friend from Nebraska, Amelia Breinig, come over. Amelia would end up joining our church and would give our daughter, Lulu, swim lessons, helping her overcome her fear of the water so she could be baptized. Amelia would end up inviting her roommate Sarah Meier from Wyoming to the church and she would later join and play keyboard in our worship band.

We had also connected with a couple of summer Hill interns from Texas, both of which would be leaving D.C. to go home the week before our first service. Great leaders understand that you plan not just for immediate need but for future growth as well. The Lord used them to encourage Autumn and I greatly in the months before there was a church. The Lord would eventually bring both of these individuals back to the city to serve at Waterfront and one of them, Bailee Dover, would end up heading up hospitality for our late service, while her husband, Austin, greets, counts and carries the podium up the stage just before the sermon each week.

Lastly, present at the game, but not with our group were Jordan and Casi Long . We had been told about this amazing couple who were leaders in another church in the area but who had been feeling that God might want them to help our church get started. When we sat down at the game that night, guess who was about 5 rows in front of us? The Longs! It was the first time Autumn and I would ever see them. I think it is fitting that Jordan and Casi are present even though they were not officially part of the team at that point because they would end up being present at just about everything our church has ever done since then. They lead a small group, have worked with the youth ministry, and lead our yearly mission effort in Slovakia. Jordan would be our first baptism, our first deacon chairman, and our first Waterfront Church local board member. They are pure gold—heaven sent to Waterfront Church–and it all started that night. I thank God regularly for sending them to us.

Can you believe it? God was hard at work in what seemed like just a baseball game. One of my favorite verses is Jeremiah 29:11. "For I know the plans I have for you, declares the Lord, plans to prosper you and not to harm you, plans to give you hope and a future." I've probably read and quoted that verse a thousand times in my life, but this day the Lord grabbed my attention in a new way with the first 5 words. FOR I KNOW THE PLANS.

God knows what He's doing. He's guiding the ship. He's building his church. He's not lying dormant, He's steadfast in his work. He's not winging it or clumsy, He's the master artist, dipping His brush deep in faith to bring about an unparalleled, complex masterpiece for the ages and that's what our new creation is. It is a complex masterpiece screaming God's favor and passion for Waterfront Church and the people in our community! If we only knew what he was up to that night. Thank you Lord for knowing the plans. And then, with the addition of our new friends in the city, now there were 24! Our little church was growing!

Chapter 16:
Hard Decisions

ave you ever had a stretch of time in your life where every day was prolifically important? This stretch was like that for me. It's bizarre. Even as I sift through journals writing this, it is hard to believe that so much happened in such a short amount of time. In stretches like these, a disciple can rarely be cognizant that they are firmly in God's grasp in the midst of every single decision (mostly because their head is spinning), even though God is certainly in complete control. I remember studying the Passion week for the first time and being in complete awe that Jesus endured so much in such a short amount of time. His exhaustion adds a whole new dimension to the intensity of that week as well as new insight into just how loved we are.

What Christ endured is so far beyond anything I ever will, but I did get a glimpse of what faith in the midst of intense complexity looks like. Not long after arriving in D.C., while during the first days of the church, my Dad left the hospital in Lubbock to see a specialist. I'll be honest, the hospital was not a surprise to us. Dad had lived on the road for two decades while traveling from town to town as an evangelist. His diet consisted mostly of gas station coffee and Allsups burritos. Years ago, there was a Saturday Night Live character played by Chris Farley called 'Matt Foley, motivational speaker.' If he had a beard, that would have been Dad! When he ended up in the hospital, our family thought to ourselves that this was likely the flashing yellow light from God telling Dad it was finally time to slow down from his unmatched pace of life. Dad's father had experienced his first heart attack around this time when he was Dad's age. Thus, about a month after moving to D.C., every night I would call Texas and get an update on Dad's testing. Everything seemed super vague, but it was about to get real.

Church planters like any entrepreneur, typically have to find work to do for extra money for a time, so they can fund their dream for a time. Our situation was no different. To make some extra money so we could afford to live in the city, I took a job preaching for 5 days at a youth camp in the Houston area for some central Texas Baptist churches. I have had the privilege to preach for a couple dozen camps over the years, but this one will always burn in my memory. I had just landed in Houston by myself. Autumn and the kids were still acclimating to the city. I got my rental car and began my 2-hour drive to the camp when my phone began to buzz in my pocket. My mom and Dad were both on the line and they asked me to pull over.

Dad had gone through another test, and this one had found something. Cancer. And not just any cancer, but cancer in his pancreas and liver. If I'm being honest, I didn't know the seriousness of what I was being told, and I truly doubt Dad did either. I had known people who had beaten cancer before, but they didn't have pancreatic cancer. Almost every other form of cancer has seen drastic strides forward in treatment over the past 40 years, but not pancreatic cancer. It is tough to tackle because it kills so quickly and painfully. Thank God I didn't know all of that on that day. "What do we do next?" I asked. Dad's reply was true wisdom. "Your mom and I are headed to M.D. Anderson for follow-up options and treatment. You need to preach the gospel with all your focus on those students this week." Dad also said not to tell anyone because he didn't want a fuss over something until there was something to fuss about.

As if cancer itself wasn't enough! When we hung up the phone I was, at first, mad—both at Dad and at God. I couldn't stand his macho, 'the show must go on' attitude while he had just dropped the word 'cancer' on me. I also couldn't believe that God had given me that information while I was all alone without any kind of support system and with the orders not to talk about this boulder hanging over my head. I stopped at a famous Texas truck stop called Buckee's to get coffee and some music to listen to on the drive. Not that it matters, but I bought 2 CDs— Johnny Cash's greatest hits and Billy Joel's #1s. My goal was to block out my worry and to try to just get through the week. Johnny Cash and Billy Joel are great, but they are hardly something to immerse your mind in before you preach. That became evident about 2 songs in. I felt even more alone in the noise. I also got no cell service in that part of the state because Autumn had just changed our cell plan when we moved to D.C. I couldn't have talked to anyone if I had tried—except to God!

Again, I pulled over on the side of the road, and this time I wept. I cried out to God, "Why? It was just getting good with him!" The past 5 years with my Dad had been what I had always dreamed of. We were best friends and partners in ministry. He valued my opinion, and I knew he respected me. His preaching, as good as it was before, had even been improving. He and the Lord were closer than they had ever been. And what if he died from this? That was the first time this thought crossed my mind. He could die soon. I quickly dismissed the thought without much reason. It was in that moment it hit me—I wasn't alone. And the timing of the news getting to me could not have been by accident. God wanted me to get the news with his words alone to comfort me. I clung to God in desperation. My mouth went from speaking accusations at God to crying out with every ounce of my soul—"What would you have me do, Master?" The Spirit brought one word to my mind—preach. That's why I was in Houston. To preach the message of Jesus Christ to students. To proclaim that no matter how deep, dark and difficult this world becomes that in Jesus we have hope!

That week, I was a wreck, but God carried me through. I was so emotional that the worship leader that week, a dear friend named Jamison Strain, pulled me aside to encourage me. So many kids were coming forward to be saved and the spirit was moving powerfully, but I was crying through every session. I broke down and told him what I was carrying. He was a preacher's kid too and understood the need to keep things under wraps. When I told him, he wept with me. We prayed each day together that week. Jamie, if you are reading this, thank you. I'll never forget your helping me carry the load that week. By the time I got back home, I could hear the Lord so clearly.

I can thank God now for those days alone, even though they seemed cruel at first. I would need to hear God clearly with what was to come. By the day I was flying home, Dad had gotten word from M.D. Anderson that he was not a candidate for surgery, and thus, if he attempted chemotherapy that he would have less than a 4% chance of living longer than 6 months. The chemo they wanted him to do was pretty brutal too, just to have a shot at the 4%. How could this have happened, and so quickly? Dad said he needed time to pray, and I told him that I would start looking at flights for Autumn, myself and the kids to spend time with him in Lubbock the next week. I knew it was serious when he agreed. But he did throw in—"Make sure they are round trip tickets, not one-way tickets."

When I got back to our apartment in D.C., Autumn was already packing us. She was so kind and diligent. Remember, cell phone service had been spotty that week at camp, and she had been forced to grieve alone in a place where she didn't know many people. As God had comforted and directed me, so he had done the same with her. Just before our trip back to Lubbock, Dad called and asked to be put on speaker phone for Autumn to hear as well. His words still amaze me. "I'm going to do the chemo, and not because I'm afraid to die. My soul is set. I'm going to do the chemo because God told me to do the chemo, and it's not my time yet." Such great wisdom.

Actions of faith motivated by fear are very weak, but actions of faith motivated by our devotion to Christ carry a holy strength. So, we went back to Lubbock for a week, after a month in D.C., and less than two months from our first Sunday service at Waterfront Church. Torn doesn't begin to describe how we felt. I journaled every day through that week totaling around 70 pages. I documented everything we did and just about everything Dad said. It won't ever be published because it's a bit raw for public consumption.

I was broken that week and all I could hear in my quiet times with God was my own pleading, "Lord, I'll follow you, but first let me bury my father!" It was the pleading of the disciple in Luke 9. I've heard that passage preached over the years with emphasis put on the speculation that this man's father was years from death and seeking to fulfill a social obligation over his calling. That's not how I read that passage anymore. I lived it. Jesus says to the man, "Let the dead bury their own dead, but you go and proclaim the kingdom." Most scholars agree that the passage that immediately follows Jesus' words here is the story of Jesus calming the storm. A sudden, unanticipated geological event that God has set in motion. The clock is ticking on this miracle and they must go NOW, or they will miss it. This miracle is so awesome and so powerful that the disciples who have been following Jesus say "Who is this man? Even the wind and the waves obey him."

For the first time, I read the passage with new eyes. Jesus was not scolding the man, he was pleading with him, not to miss a once in a lifetime collision with almighty God. It became clear that God was not scolding me either—telling me to buck up and get back to work—he was pleading with me to cling to him and to trust the vision he gave all those years ago. The miracle could not be rescheduled. I believe the story of Waterfront Church was written before time began and orchestrated by the mind of our God. Every Sunday is a miracle, and this was the moment we almost removed ourselves from the vision. The Holy Spirit compels the divided heart of the visionary—Don't miss the miracle! Proclaim the kingdom! I knew that last night that we couldn't stay in Lubbock with Dad. We had to go. We had to see this God-given thing through.

The next morning, Dad started his first round of chemo and I went with him while Autumn packed for the airport. He looked nervous, like a kid on the first day of school, but he quickly made friends and started witnessing for Christ right there in the chemo room. Classic Dad. We sat together a long time. His chemo stretches were 6-8 hours a pop and brutal. I took every second right up to our flight time to be with him. The last hour, I couldn't stop crying. The tears just flowed like water from a faucet. I finally got the courage to tell him that we had to go back to D.C., and that we would be staying there. He crinkled his brow and said, "You were thinking of staying? Why? You can't throw away your vision. I wouldn't have let you come back even if you had wanted to."

He understood God's timing too. The concept of Lordship is key when pursuing a vision. What sits on the throne of your life? When the really hard calls come, who gets to make the decision? The answer to both questions for the disciple has the be Jesus. So, we boarded the plane and headed back to D.C. with faith that a miracle was coming that we did not need to miss. God would not disappoint.

Chapter 17:
God Can Do It

I n the game of blackjack, one of the most exhilarating moments takes place when you get dealt an 11 by the dealer. At this point, if the dealer is still in the game, all of the strategy books tell you to 'double down,' which is essentially doubling your bet by only taking one more card in hopes of doubling your winnings. The magic number you are trying to reach is 21 without going over. The odds are in your favor with 11 because there are more 10-point cards in the deck than any other number, but if you had already bet big that hand, the wrong card after an 11 could hurt you and at the very least, greatly set back your progress.

New creations are filled with double-down moments, some of which you will need to let pass. There is no rule in black-jack that you have to double down, and there is no rule in ministry or business that you have to either. However, when the Spirit of God calls for it, you've got to have the guts to trust him—the rewards for that kind of faith are huge! God knows the figurative cards that are being dealt your way. When he says bet big, we should faithfully bet big. That is so easy to say and so very difficult to do. Thank God for the Holy Spirit's conviction.

Not long after returning to D.C. from our trip to see Dad in Lubbock, I was spending some time in prayer one morning and felt the Spirit's leading to double down on something. In the process of putting our church planting strategy together, we had read a lot of books on the subject. Books by leaders like Aubrey Malphurs, Mark Batterson, and Nelson Sercey were so important in forming our strategy. In fact, Nelson Sercey's book "Launch," in many ways, served as the nuts and bolts template for our church plant. The insight from those books was truly heaven sent to us, but I say that with a heavy caution.

There is no book other than the Bible that should carry the same weight as the voice of the Holy Spirit in your life, especially in relation to your new creation. Even this one. Early on, pioneers of a new creation can find strength and wisdom in analyzing the twists and turns of another successful person's journey, but in the end, it must be the Holy Spirit guiding your glorious journey and not you duplicating someone else's, hoping for similar results. I can only speak for the area of church planting but hear me clearly— THERE IS NO PERFECT FORMULA TO ENSURE A SUCCESSFUL CHURCH PLANT, other than by God's divine leading and provision.

I would guess that the same is true of any entrepreneurial venture. The creative genius behind your vision is God himself, and it has been my experience, God does not desire to give glory to a system when it is his unmatched mind that deserves it. That being said, many of the books we read and the testimonies we heard in relation to urban church planting offered the advice to begin the church's life with monthly services and weekly small group meetings. The idea was to slow launch the services and place the focus on community gatherings. We, of course, value small groups greatly. It is the most effective way for people to meet one another and genuinely connect in a growing church.

It also alleviated our fundraising a bit because of the $1100/week price tag for us to rent the 2nd floor of the Courtyard Marriott Hotel. Our original plan was to do monthly services for the first five months starting August 10, 2014, and then ease into weekly meetings in January 2015. That meant that doing monthly services in the beginning would save us $18,600. That's a lot of money when the church didn't even exist yet. The Holy Spirit had other plans. A few of the people we had met in our apartment building had shown great interest in joining our church but stopped short of joining our launch team saying, "Just let me know when your first service is and then afterwards, I'll tell you if I will be able to join." Image in D.C. is a huge concern. You can be hurt not just by the person you are but by the people you are connected to. They were kindly saying, I won't commit to you until I know you. Honestly, I get it. The Holy Spirit should be our ultimate guide, but many of these people were not Christians, and they were nervous that they could be attaching themselves to a southern kook seeking to push a new political ideology in the capital city.

Many had done it before, and they were wise to that move. In my time of prayer, the Holy Spirit brought to light that we needed to do weekly services from the beginning. I know what some of you are thinking—how did the Spirit 'talk' to you? In moments of prayer we hear from God through what scripture calls a "still small voice." I do this by praying, thanking God for what he's done, reading scripture and then clearing my mind and asking, "God, what would you have me do?" I then wait for thoughts and ideas to rush into my mind that I know did not come from me, followed by a spiritual fist in my gut cementing that I will not be able to move about freely in my day until I've done what the spirit has cast vision for me to do.

Just for the record, you know when a thought comes from you. It's usually in the form of a daily to-do list, but when it comes from God, it is usually oddly specific and something that was vaguely on your radar, if it was on the radar at all. This particular morning the spirit had been clear that we needed to do weekly services and not monthly services. Fear hit me like lightning. We had not budgeted for it. We had made a different plan. Would our launch team think I was a poor leader if we changed direction this close to our first day? Would the Marriott still be available? Would anyone even show up to the first service? These were legitimate concerns, but also legitimate distractions from what I'd been commanded to do.

That week, about a month out of our August 10th launch date, I called the core of our church together (which was at that time was only me, my wife, our worship leader and his wife) and told them what I'd been experiencing and what I felt like we were being called to do. All three were skeptical, even my own wife! All the turmoil with Dad's cancer, the struggle of getting moved across the country, and the overarching fear that no one was going to come to our first service was overwhelming. And to two families that had truly left everything in pursuit of a dream that could one day eventually sustain their salaries, $18,600 seemed like money out of their pockets—including my own family. It is of note here that my wife and I had made a commitment to recruit money for the church and all of its expenses rather than fundraising our salary separately.

Many church planters recruit their salary first and then plant with what's left. We always felt like that would give us a reason to quit early in fundraising. I have no judgement for those who recruit their salaries first, but for me, our personal money came after the church got its funding. Think of it like giving God our first fruits. For the record, balancing

133

the tightrope of taking care of my family and taking care of the church have not been even close to perfect in my life and ministry. I lean toward work-a-holism and am learning to submit to God in the areas of work and family.

On this day however, my struggle proved a strength. I'll never forget telling the team, and immediately, they were hesitant, and seriously, I didn't blame them. Our worship leader's wife was willing to do whatever was best for the team but wondered why there was such a sudden change. Autumn, who knew the finances better than anyone at this point, was cautious that we really think this through because gobs of money were going out and nothing was really coming in apart from our current pledges. Our worship leader was concerned about our set up and tear down team getting burned out. Portable Church is a massive undertaking, and on the scale we were attempting, it could not be done alone. All valid points. All valid concerns. But the Spirit had spoken, and we needed to have faith.

That being said, I did not issue an edict that day that we were going to weekly services. I knew it would take time for them to process, just as it had been a need for me. So, I asked them to pray about it and then said we would meet the following week to talk about what God had said to them. This was one of the first truly pastoral moments in our young church's history. When we reconvened to talk through the decision the following week, it was clear that this was what we needed to do, even though the group was not necessarily unanimous. And that was ok.

Leaders who wait for a unanimous consensus with their new creation will find themselves constantly waiting. God has sent the visionary leader to inspire courage and the rational leader to inspire process. They need each other and they need respect for one another. So, we moved forward together, committing $18,600 we did not have to a congregation we hoped would exist. My prayers that week were simple—Lord, send us reaffirmation. I will often tell God that I'm fully on board with his plan, but any encouragement he chooses to provide will be greatly celebrated and appreciated.

The very next day after this meeting, Autumn and I went to our church's P.O. Box at the Southwest Station in D.C. to get the mail. We even prayed in the parking lot before we went in that God would encourage us in our decision to spend this extra money to reach more people with the Gospel. In the midst of the junk mail there was a letter from a woman in Amarillo, TX, we had never met. She was a friend of Dwain and Bobby Sue Walker, two of the sweetest people in the entire world from our church in Lubbock. Dwain was the head greeter at the church and currently working as a driver for Enterprise Rent-A-Car. Bobby Sue was like the church mama, and a ray of sunshine to anyone she was around. They were both in their 70s and on their second marriages due to deceased spouses. They were not wealthy, but so, so generous. They were not power chasers, but quite influential. They were the embodiment of what Christlike servants should be.

In the letter, the woman said that Bobby Sue had brought copies of our launch plan brochures to their WMU gathering at their church. She had told them about us and asked if anyone would be willing to help us reach D.C. with the Gospel. Enclosed was a check for $7,500. I wept, and so did Autumn. That was almost half of what we had needed for the weekly services. And the best part was that God had provided it through someone we had never met—a friend of a friend who caught the vision. God has all the money in the world at his disposal. He will not withhold it from the faithful when they strive to courageously carry out the mission!

God would end up providing way more than $18,600. All of a sudden the vision was evolving in me, and my faith in what God could do was growing. My Dad was also experiencing some wins as well. His oncologist had put together a plan of action to blitz Dad's system with chemo treatments. Despite all his setbacks, my Dad had one major thing other than the hand of God in his favor: He had been born with an iron stomach. Dad only threw up a handful of times throughout his chemotherapy despite a truly brutal regiment that would have leveled anyone else. We talked almost every night, and his favorite thing was to talk ministry. He hated talking about the cancer. We gave him updates on all of our miracles, and he gave us updates on all of his. That stretch was so intense but looking back, it was so encouraging as well. "God can do anything he wants to do," I remember thinking. He can build a church from nothing but his thoughts. Could he heal my father too?

It was my deepest wish. I prayed for it multiple times a day alongside the prayer for our church to exist. It is why the two are so melded together in our story. My friends, I can tell you honestly that God is faithful. He is so very faithful. He heard every prayer, and I could feel his presence like never before. I was changing. God had given this amazing vision for the new creation that would be Waterfront Church, but he was revealing a new level to his plan—that I would change. I began to understand that I was the new creation God had started fashioning all those years ago kneeling at the foot of my futon in Stillwater, OK. God had placed me firmly in the crucible, and I could feel his hands reforming my spirit. I would never be the same after these days, and I was going to be ready launch day.

Chapter 18:
Prepare for Launch

Watching a new creation take life is a lot like watching the birth of a child, and honestly, my wife and I talk about Waterfront like it is our fifth kid. When we were in the final weeks leading up to our church's first service (we were calling it Launch Day), the day I prayed at the foot of my futon while a student at Oklahoma State seemed so far away. Yet, the calling to see this thing through could not be stronger. Would anyone come? Would there be a church to pastor? I found great solace in the 30 mission team people from Indiana Ave Baptist Church, along with several of our board members and their friends that were coming to add body count just in case no one came. For those of you planting a church remember that there is a correct number to seed with, so the room is not empty, but doesn't look false.

We had a group of 200 offer to come seed our first Sunday, but we knew it was a bad idea. If the crowd had gone from 200 to 20 between week one and week two, it would have sent a message to the repeat attendees that week one was not indicative of what they could expect. 30 extra was just right, no matter who showed. The second floor of the Courtyard Marriott was made up of 3 rooms with collapsible walls between them that we were using for a 150-seat worship and one isolated room that we were using for the kid's space for kids 5 and under. Altogether, the rooms were about 2,100 square feet. Connecting them all was a long hallway with bathrooms at one end and stairs and an elevator at the other. Lining the south side of the rooms were windows overlooking the growing neighborhood with the sounds of the city in the background.

It was not the ideal place to preach because in order to get to 150 seats in there, you had to put the pulpit in the middle of the rooms. This meant that while preaching, your back was always to someone, and the people on the sides were staring straight at each other the entire service. That seriously was my only complaint.. The space was perfect for a new church, and right smack in the middle of where God had called us to be. I still thank God regularly for the Marriott and for our sales associate, Amelia, who took a chance on us.

I've done a lot of things over the years that warranted being nervous, but in the weeks leading up the launch, I don't know that I've ever been that nervous in my entire life. Just about every church planter has the same nightmare in the days leading up to the first service. For me, they even continued all throughout the first year of our church's existence. I repeatedly dreamed that it's Sunday morning, the music starts, and my family and I are sitting on the front row singing. During the final song, before getting up to preach the message, I turn to see an empty auditorium and my wife in tears.

It doesn't take much psychoanalysis to dissect that dream. I was fearful that our work and sacrifice would be in vain and that no one would show up. Even after launch day, the dream continued because I was worried no one would come back! This experience helped me learn the difference between a God-given vision and a stupid nightmare. One is a promise from God and the other is a product from your insecurities. Don't get me wrong—there is plenty you need to be doing to via connecting with people and marketing to best ensure your room is not empty, but after legitimately doing all you can, you have to trust that God will not leave you hanging when you put yourself out there in his name. After each nightmare I would pray, "Please Lord, fill the room." It was a great reminder that God was working even harder than we were and that very soon ... he would indeed fill the room!

The week before the launch was a whirlwind. We did every-thing imaginable to let people know a service was about to happen and a church was being born. You can still go online and watch the Facebook video that one of our launch team members, Jadi Chapman (now Jadi Romero—she married her husband Jeff after meeting him at Waterfront), shot of me in our meeting space with empty chairs. I almost seem like I'm begging for people to try us out. In truth, I was. The hunger and desperation for people to come and hear the message of Jesus is something we should never lose. Mission teams came from all over the country to help us guerrilla market, and we really did try just about anything. We Facebook marketed, we mailed out to 15,000 households, we handed out thousands of water bottles with our logo and service info on the labels, and we canvased D.C. homes with about 30,000 door hangers.

Jacob West and his team from FBC Stamford even threw a shrimp boil party for our apartment building where dozens came for free food in the church's name. Jacob would later confess that he'd never done a shrimp boil before but was happy to try one on our prospects. It was awesome. Some of you reading this might ask if this was truly mission work. Are you kidding me? God honors sacrifice, especially when it is the stuff anyone can do. Our humility is a spotlight on God's power. The selflessness of the mission teams to serve in D.C. by doing things they could have stayed home to do was powerfully humble, and the Lord honored their sacrifice on Launch Day.

On the day before the launch, there was only one thing left to do. We had asked the Marriott for some extra time on Saturday night so we could get the room perfect for the following morning. We established our first setup crew and I asked our team to do a full-dress rehearsal that night. We would go through all the songs, I'd preach, and we'd make sure there were no hiccups with the sound, etc. If you are planning a launch on any level, I highly encourage a dress rehearsal. We found so many holes, and our people felt great ownership in helping. Remember, often people offer criticism not because they are displeased, but because they are looking for a way to become part of the team. Not always, but often.

Rod and Jennifer Johnson, our friends from Texas, were there and asked us if we had a video camera to document this historic day. That had not even crossed my mind, even though it should have. Thanks to the two of them, there are videos of our first services and this rehearsal. When it came time to do the offering, we noticed that there were no baskets to pass. This was critical because we were having everyone fill out a visitor card on Sunday and there was nothing to collect them with. Dwain and Bobby Sue Walker, the sweet couple from last chapter, had come in to help us that weekend and offered to get offering baskets. We still have them today.

David Godfrey had also flown in from Texas for the first service. We had 2 TV's for the three rooms, and it was a bit awkward. He pulled out his checkbook and said, "How much for you to get a third tv and a stand for next week?" The following week we had 3 TV's. He also noticed a major hole in our setup model. I had stubbornly fought against getting a trailer to haul our church equipment because there was nowhere close to park it in the city, but after seeing how much work it was going to be, David also offered to buy us a trailer. We later would find a farmer in north Texas to donate a truck to pull the trailer. God was providing at every turn! That night, you could see the tension on my face, and you could feel the anticipation building.

We prayed and prayed that night for a miracle. Would it come? I was a different man than I was even weeks before. I called Dad that night after everyone else was asleep. I told him I was scared. It seems silly now. He was dying of cancer, and I was the scared one. "They'll come," he said kindly. "God has written this story."

My eyes fill with tears as I write this part. He was right. He was so encouraging. Even when his body had been blasted with chemo, he was still so unbelievably encouraging. "I don't think I'll sleep much tonight," I told him. "I'd worry about you if you did," he quipped. "I doubt Joshua slept before they marched around Jericho." He prayed for me as my pastor that night. It was like a true passing of the torch. "Call me as soon as you get home tomorrow. I want to hear about what God did."

Chapter 19:
A Church is Born!

barely slept. In fact, I've often looked back on August 9 and August 10, 2014, as one single day. It felt like my entire life had been building to this moment. I had been created to serve God and to love him with my whole heart, just like everyone on this earth, but this new creation, Waterfront Church, was truly a part of my destiny. I remember praying everywhere that morning. I prayed in my bed, at the foot of my bed, in the shower, at the breakfast table, in the apartment lobby, in my walk to the hotel, and all through setup. We scheduled the service for 10 a.m. but I got up there about 3 hours early just in case. Everything looked perfect.

As the launch team rolled in, you could feel that many of them had experienced the same night I had. At one point just before the start of the service, I ran to the restroom and almost threw up. The mission team from Texas that week was so helpful. Indiana Avenue Baptist Church from Lubbock, Texas, was there, and they had offered to staff every volunteer need so that our D.C. team could all be in the very first service. It was so special. We were still almost an hour from the start of the service and almost 50 people, including the mission team, were walking the halls. It would not be an empty room! Those nightmares had truly been a lie from the devil. Not only that, but the people were so happy to be together. This would become a staple characteristic of Waterfront Church. We love being together.

As the clock got closer to 10 a.m., the most exciting thing happened—people I didn't know started coming into the room, and they all looked so different! This would become another staple characteristic of Waterfront Church. There was honest diversity in the room on every level. Our church skewed younger, but there were people with different skin colors, different ages, and different economic statuses all spread out through the room and all led here in some way by the Holy Spirit. When the music started, I had to fight back my tears. It was happening! The Lord was being worshipped in D.C.! A Church was being born! Behold, a new creation taking its first breath in the world! I'm still overwhelmed to think about it. I lifted my hands in worship praising God for what he had done.

When I finally got up to preach. I introduced myself to the people. It is ironic, now— a pastor who was also a first-time visitor at his own church. I told them about my family and did my best to cast a vision for what our church would be if they would only come with us in the journey. I preached the first Waterfront Church message from Luke 12. It was on the subject of Godly momentum, and what Jesus says to his disciples before addressing the crowds that were literally stepping on one another to get to Jesus. He tells the disciples to avoid gossip, fearing what people think, and trying to go through life alone. I told them that this was the kind of church we were trying to build and that if we succeeded then, we could reach the masses stepping on one another to get to Jesus. It was a spirit-filled moment. The people listened and then we went into our first time of public prayer (we call it our time of reflection).

A church planting mentor of mine, Cody Whitfill, offered some amazing advice for the very first church service. Cody had great wisdom because he also had planted a church that had grown greatly from what started as a vision from God. Cody said, "At the end of your first service, ask for people to commit to give you four weeks." What a great word of advice. This not only gave them some ownership, but it shepherded them through what the Holy Spirit was doing in their hearts. At the end of the service, I had them bow their heads, we prayed and then I asked them who would be willing to give our church the next four weeks. To my amazement, 25-30 D.C. residents raised their hands. God was building his church. We would not have an empty room next week either! At that point, I did cry. When we closed the service, hardly anyone left. It was bizarre. The congregation was gelling together like old friends.

Two of our neighbors were at the service that day—Bertie Ruffin and Michelle Hugee, who would embody the spirit of Waterfront Church. The two are now known as our 'hugging ladies'. They head up our welcome team and have set the tone for visitors from the moment they step on campus that Waterfront Church is a place where you will be valued. Both are heroes of the faith as far as I'm concerned, and God sent them on day one. Michelle heard about our church from a door hanger and Bertie famously received a Waterfront Church water bottle in front of the CVS one afternoon. They are living examples of what happens when mission team sacrifice is in the hands of the Holy Spirit. God also sent Brian and Tara Campbell to the service. They have been faithful members, and Tara's parents are now small group leaders at our church.

That was also the day we met Charlene Trechenburg. She was a lovely woman, originally from Taiwan, that had worked at the Pentagon for decades. She would end up hosting our first college ministry gatherings among a thousand other things. She was in her mid60's and so full of life. She encouraged Autumn and I often, and she defended our young church as viciously as I would have to predators. Her funeral would end up being the second in our church's history. She was heaven sent to us for a time. At the end of the first day, the count was in. 104 people attended the service and 84 of those were D.C. residents. 84! We had begged God for 25. He is truly able to do abundantly more than we could ever ask or imagine! What could God possibly do next?

We packed up the church that afternoon, and the celebration continued. The people from Texas that had come in for the service were hugging me and giving praise to God. I can still remember the voice of Stan Gill, a man I'd known since childhood, speaking encouragement that God was establishing something for the ages that day. We felt it too. Once everything was done, I went back to our apartment, two blocks from the church (yes, to us, it was no longer the Marriott but the church), and our kids had all been put down for a nap. Autumn was on the couch grinning.

"We did it," she said. Now before you get legalistic and say that she was wrong because God did it, come off your high horse and realize what she was saying—we had the faith to see it through. God did the miracle, but we faithfully followed him in the face of incredible adversity. "We did it," I said as I sat next to her on our couch and wept again.

My phone exploded with a hundred texts from pastors and donors asking about the day. I must have texted the number 84 until my fingers hurt. I called my Dad shortly after this because he was in the central time zone and still preaching. Dad hardly missed preaching a single Sunday during chemo. He was so proud but not at all surprised. The only sad point came when he said, "Well, I guess now you have to stay." He was not hoping for us to fail. In fact, very much the opposite, but a bad day might have pushed us back his direction. That moment brought us to a new point of heavenly understanding—God was still forming his new creation and this day was only the beginning.

One good service was not God's aim. A church that would outlive its founding pastor was his aim. A church that would disciple and deploy his people was his aim. A church that would cling to the truths of scripture no matter what politics are in play was his aim. A church broken for those in need and sacrificially helping them was his aim. We still had work to do. That was truly the day D.C. became home for me. I knew that Texas would always be my roots, but that it would be a long time before we could claim Texas soil again, if ever. I put my hand to the plow that day and refused to look back. Dad closed our conversation saying, "I want to see your church with my own eyes." He'd been given weeks to live. I never dreamed that would be possible. His odds were so slim. But we were in a season of miracles! On August 10, 2014, the word impossible seemed to lose its meaning. Maybe, just maybe, he would see the church. God could certainly do it. I'd learned that much. And then there were 84. To God be the glory, great things he hath done!

Chapter 20:
A Season of Healing

Have you ever felt 'on a roll' before? The idea is that you are in a season where everything just seems to fall into place right where it needs to be. Now, we as believers in Jesus Christ know that God is the one lining things up, but the seasons are precious when there are very few speed bumps on our crazy faith journey. I believe God allows this for a time to develop courage and confidence. Both are very Godly traits when developed properly with the right perspective.

After our launch day on August 10, 2014, we entered a season of being on a roll in just about every area. After launch day, we settled in at about 60 D.C. residents in attendance at the church. That was fairly unheard of in a lot of the urban church planting circles we ran in. When our church was about a month old, we held our first ever membership class and had 28 charter members join the church. Four of those needed to be baptized, which posed a new question—where would we baptize people? There are lots of ways to baptize people in a portable church context, but none of them are very simple. I was baptized in a swimming pool in Oklahoma when I was younger and so my mind immediately went to seek the Courtyard Marriott swimming pool, also on the second floor, as an option.

I was initially nervous about the conversation with our Courtyard Marriott contact, Amelia. The idea of asking for a religious ritual to be performed in the company pool seemed like it would be a stretch. True to the season, God worked everything out perfectly. She had no problem with us using the pool for baptism, "as long as it was between the hours of 11:00 a.m. and 11:30 a.m. on Sundays when it was being serviced. That time fit perfectly for us to baptize at the end of the service. Only God could have had the pool available exactly when we needed it. Our first baptism was Jordan Long (our first deacon chairman and Waterfront board member), our second was Josiah Gross (the head of our media ministry and all round behind-the-scenes hero), our third was Kylie Mills (our church's first Salvation), and fourth was our worship leader's wife, baptized by her husband. It was a really special day!

We also started to see volunteer signups increase so that the children's ministry workers, like my wife, got to go to services on a rotation rather than working in the kid's area every week. Our setup and tear down teams were growing and getting the trailer was a huge hit with them! People rarely missed anything we did in the early days because there was so much excitement in being part of something that was happening for the first time. Then came the crazy day that CJ Monroe called. CJ had been part of the mission team from Texas that was with us on Launch Day. He had been our media director that day, running slides for the worship lyrical and sermon notes. He called about a month after that day and said the Lord had told him to move to D.C. to help us. My initial response was, "But, we don't have any money." He said, "If I raised it, could you use my help?"

I was perplexed. D.C. is not cheap. I told him we'd love to have him if he was up for raising it. Four months later, he was on our team, and a gift from God to our church and specifically to me. It was tough to give CJ a title because he just did anything and everything the Church needed at the time. God truly know what you need before you ask him. Our community events were growing too. More and more people were finding out about our church and more and more people were coming on board. We finished 2014 averaging just over 77 people a week, and the Church was remaining strong in its diversity.

In fact, in some ways it was expanding. Our church is strategically placed. If you go a mile north of our campus, you run into Capitol Hill and some of the wealthiest and most powerful people in the world. If you go a mile south, you hit Anacostia and some of the most impoverished people on the East Coast. We say this regularly at our church: Jesus is the bridge between politics and poverty. We are all sinners saved by grace through the shed blood of Jesus Christ. It all of a sudden became common to see a congressional official sitting next to someone who had been homeless in our services. The first time I noticed, I almost started to cry. It is a glimpse of heaven. One particular Sunday in my memory, both a homeless man and a congressman sitting next to him tithed in the same service. It was awesome.

But the blessings didn't just stop there. Dad was also experiencing some victory. It worked in less than 4% of his particular cases, and the chemo was working!!! Dad was also gaining a bit of courage and confidence himself. He was preaching every week like it was his last, fighting to keep standing like a battered prize fighter and many were coming to Christ. He had become a new creation. He spoke the powerful words of wisdom he had always possessed, but now had the look of Paul just after the shipwreck, failed stoning, and prison malnourishment. He lived what he preached. Truly. There was also a gentleness to him that had not been there before. He was still fiery, but gentle, and God kept adding time to his clock.

He became the subject of many conversations from Texas to D.C. How was he surviving? Was the preacher healed? How long would it last? One thing was for certain during that stretch—if you were anywhere near him, you wanted to make time to hear him preach. December brought unthinkable joy. Dad called and said, "Listen, my battle is not over, but they think they are going to declare me cancer free." We were shocked. From weeks to live to cancer free. How? Only God. He cautioned, "This is not remission, but just a sign that the chemo is working, and God has given me more time." That week, I told the church the good news. They were so happy for my family, and then two of the Congressmen in our church, Randy Neugabauer from our town in Texas, and Mark Meadows from North Carolina, came up and said, "Would your Dad be willing to come up and pray to open a session of Congress?" I was ecstatic! We put together a timeline and organized it so Dad could come into D.C. with a mission team from his church in Texas on the second Saturday in March 2015.

He would preach at Waterfront Church in our (now) 2 services on Sunday, and then preach a conference for us. We were calling it the Think Conference on Sunday, Monday, and Tuesday nights, praying at the Capitol Tuesday morning. Dad would preach the first revival in our church's history. I'd never heard anyone better. Congressman Neugebauer made all the arrangements at the Capitol, and our people waited with great anticipation to see the cancer-defying prophet come to the miracle church in the District. Courage and confidence abounded during those precious months. We would need all of it for what lie ahead.

Chapter 21:
God's Timing is Perfect

The older I get and the further I get into our faith journey with this new creation, the more I realize how grateful I am to not know the future. Don't get me wrong, I know THE future—I'll spend eternity with God in heaven because of my relationship with Jesus Christ. That's the ultimate end for all who believe in him. But I'm grateful that God holds our future in our time on this planet, and that we don't know how things will unfold until they unfold. Even a vision like the one I had back in Stillwater doesn't tell you all of what you will be navigating. It is actually incredibly kind of God to withhold those heavy details. He carries them for us when he knows they could crush us. God was very gracious to carry Dad's end date. Had any of us known, we might have ruined the glorious finale.

It was the beginning of March, less than a week before Dad was supposed to land in D.C. We were so excited. There was a buzz around the church about the Think Conference and last-minute arrangements were being made. My phone rang late in the evening after the kids had gone to bed. It was Dad. "Hey, pops!" I said. I always called Dad pops when we were in informal settings. "Hey, son. Can you put me on speaker phone with Autumn? I need to tell you both something." Autumn came in sat down.. Dad had been having some trouble after a surgery he had on one of his liver spots. It had caused him to lose some weight, but it seemed like no big deal compared to what he'd already been through.

I remember he led by asking how many we had on Sunday at our service. "The weather was bad, and we still broke 100, pops! It was a great day! Are you ok, pops?"

His voice was so gentle and steady. "I need to tell you something. This past Saturday, I had one of the best days of my life. Your mother and I spent the morning together, I went out on the porch with the dogs for a long while, the sun was shining, and I didn't hurt like I've been hurting recently. It was truly just a great day. I thank God for that great day. But that night, Doctor Miller told me that the cancer is back and it's everywhere. They are saying I've probably got about 30 days left."

Dad's initial cancer had been localized to his pancreas and his liver. This time it was in his stomach too and moving very aggressively. I was broken hearted and so was Autumn. He immediately started telling me how proud he was of me and how proud he was of Autumn. I tried to tell him all the ways he has blessed my life, that he was my best friend and that I couldn't picture life without him. I could hear him crying on the other end of the phone. That call aged me a decade in a few moments. He said, "I've given you all the tools in your tool box that you'll need going forward."

That's what a good Dad does, I suppose. He can't fix things forever, but he can certainly teach you how to use the tools. God would finish the work he had used my father to begin.

"I'll call Congressman Neugebauer tomorrow and cancel the prayer and the Think Conference. We'll get a flight to Lubbock tomorrow," I said sadly. "Like heck you will," Dad said. "I'm coming to preach." I was confused. "But you're sick," I said. "I'm coming to see your church and the miracle you've been working on, and I'd never miss a chance to pray at the Capitol. You just make sure it's ready to go." It was so Dad. He was dying like he lived. Preaching the gospel until there was no breath left in his lungs. You couldn't help but admire his determination, and God used it to give me strength to endure. We prayed together, hung up the phone and then got to work. I don't remember being mad at God a single moment throughout that week. I remember being so grateful to have one more revival with him. One more fight side by side against the powers of darkness in Jesus' name. But I was still blind to what God was really doing. He was about to fulfill the vision he gave so many years before.

Chapter 22:
Old Man White Beard, Young Man Green Shirt

Word spread pretty quickly that Dad was in his final days. He was so loved. Countless friends and people he had ministered alongside over the years messaged and asked how they could help us through this difficult time. It meant the world just to be thought of. One of our friends, David Wolfe (the kind man that helped us get our car), heard that Dad was going to have difficulty getting on and off of the commercial airliner, so he called Mike Chism (one of our board member's husband) and the two of them found a private plane for Dad to fly in on. It was a great gift because that meant Dad could maneuver around without having to fight the airport crowds. He was in constant pain, and you could see it in his face.

Most private planes fly into a special terminal at Dulles Airport in D.C. It took about 40 minutes for us to drive there from our apartment on the Saturday that Dad landed. I had borrowed a wheelchair from Spotswood Baptist Church in Fredericksburg, VA, that Dad would use to get around that week. Our kiddos were in the car, and Lulu was so excited to see her Grandles. It was also about a week before Lulu's 5th birthday, so she was about to be showered with gifts. One of my favorite memories of my Dad was Christmas morning. Because he was always out preaching revivals, Christmas was one of the only times we knew we would have his full attention. By planning on giving Lulu her birthday presents after Dad got off the plane at our apartment, we effectively got one more Christmas morning together.

As we pulled up to the airport to pick Dad up. I was nervous. It had actually been months since I had seen him, even though we talked every day. He had repeatedly asked me not to come because it was hard to see me and the kids go. When he got off the plane, I was shocked. He had lost so much weight from the illness—about 60 pounds in a matter of months—but that wasn't what startled me. It was his hair. The last time I had seen Dad, he had lost his hair and beard to the chemo. Now, his hair and beard were back, but they were no longer grey and patchy— they were white! Like Gandalf from Lord of the Rings, Dad had changed. Chemo does strange things to the body, but this was not something I saw coming. He looked so happy to see us.

One of our board members, Scott Hicks, took the job pushing Dad's wheelchair. Scott was Dad's body guard for the week, and he was beyond efficient. Scott is as close to family as you can get for me. He had assumed the role of right-hand man for Dad when we moved to D.C. and I'll always be grateful. He also allowed me to be the son even though he could have made a play for that role in Dad's fragile state. For that I will always be doubly grateful. Scott is that true friend you always hope God will send your way. Dad and I got to share him that week. The 40-minute drive was awesome. I had my Dad in the car in my new city. I don't remember much of what was said, but I do remember him smiling a lot, and I remember his eyes staying closed, most likely because of the pain.

When we got to our apartment, Dad sat on our couch and we handed him gifts to hand to Lulu. It was just like Christmas morning, and you couldn't even tell he was hurting. He loved Lulu so much, and he was so proud of Jack. He would joke that he couldn't remember Harper's name by just calling her "the baby." It was all a farce because we had named Harper after his own mother. And then, all of the sudden, things took a turn. He was clearly in unmanageable pain and needed to leave. His team of Scott Hicks, David Wolfe, my mom, my sister, and my brother-in-law sprang into action. They had been his day-to-day caregivers through the really tough stretch. In that moment, I felt shame that I wasn't part of that team. It hurt that I had not been there for him. He would later reassure me that this was never meant to be my role. God had called me to be the caregiver for Waterfront Church not him.

They immediately took Dad to his hotel—you guessed it—the Courtyard Marriott where Waterfront Church met. Amelia had gotten Dad a room on the top floor over-looking the neighborhood and every hotel worker prom-ised to get him anything he needed. Being in the hotel twice a week now (we had started doing Wednesday night activities as well) meant we knew just about everyone on the payroll. Some of the employees that regularly worked Sundays would use their coffee breaks to sneak into the ser-vices. They treated Dad like family that week. Moments after getting Dad to his room, he realized that my mom had forgotten his cargo pants that he was planning on preaching in the next day. It was about 7:30 p.m. and most of the retail shops were closing and as cargo pants had gone out of style about 10 years earlier, so finding some would be a task.

Again, David Wolfe, Scott Hicks and I sprang into action, and found the last two pair of cargo pants at an American Eagle outlet in National Harbor, MD. I can still see the three of us running through the shops in my head. No one wanted to fail any task given to them that week by my old man. When we got back, Dad was asleep. He'd need his rest to preach the three services the next day. Just as we were walking out, Scott caught me and said, "Be ready to preach tomorrow, if he struggles." He explained that Dad would sometimes lose his train of thought if the pain got too bad and that I needed to be ready to intervene.

No one knew better than I did of how deeply it would hurt Dad to be put on the shelf while preaching. Like an angry pitcher sent to the showers, he would be furious and hurt. I begged God to give him strength to finish strong. That next morning, Dad was so proud to see our church in full swing. He couldn't believe it. That's one of my favorite parts about Waterfront Church—the stories, as amazing as they are, do not do it justice when you experience it for yourself. It is one thing to hear about the decisions for Christ, but when you actually meet the people, it's beyond special. It is one thing to hear about the diversity, but when you experience it, it feels like a preview of what heaven will be like. Dad just kept smiling. He leaned over to me in the worship set and said, "Son, this is a real church!" I couldn't help but smile. I knew what he meant. This wasn't just a gathering. It wasn't just a service. It was a body of believers becoming a local church. I still grin thinking about that.

When he got up to preach, it was powerful. He didn't have the energy to stand, so he preached sitting down. A lot of what he did that Sunday morning was vintage Dad. It was the stuff I'd heard him preach at revivals since I was a kid. I was so proud our people would get to experience it. He started to stumble a bit in the second service, but God was good and helped him regain composure. After the services were over, he quickly retreated to his room. There wasn't a lot of conversation that day. Sundays where you preach 3 times are hard enough when you don't have cancer. Dad would spend huge chunks of that day sleeping. My mom caught me at one point and told me, "He's giving you every-thing he has left this week." I told her that I didn't want it—that I just wanted him not to hurt. She replied, "You're his best friend. He wants to do a good job for you,, and you can't stop him." She was right. He was a beast that week.

The next day, my brother and his family came into town and we did our final set of family photos together in the Courtyard Marriott lobby next to the fireplace. Dad looked so frail from where he had been. Our photographer, Denise, had been the same photographer that took all of our early Waterfront Church shots. She was a journalistic style pho-tographer and very talented at getting the candid, real shot. She captured Dad perfectly interacting with all of us. That night we didn't quite know what to expect at the Think Conference from our Waterfront people. Would anyone come back on a Monday night for a sermon in D.C.? I'd been told over and over that revivals didn't work on the East Coast, but that night, more than 60 D.C. people came back for the service!

During the worship portion, one my favorite moments ever happened. Dad had been confined to his wheelchair through every service, but this night, as the band was playing, he would not be denied standing and worship-ping his savior. He was so weak, and with his eyes shut, he stood to his feet with his arms outstretched. Without him knowing, David Wolfe and Scott Hicks stood beside him and held his arms up, that he might call out to God in worship! It was like Joshua and Aaron standing next to Moses. The whole room was lifted to heaven. He sang until he had no strength left. One of the mission team members got a picture of it, and it is still my favorite picture ever taken. He had illustrated for our people that worship is not the songs that you sing, but rather it is the attitude of your heart.

At the end of worship, we saw a figure sneak in the back. It was Senator James Lankford from Oklahoma. Several of his staff had become Waterfront Church members (one of his Legislative assistants, Adam Farris would be one of our first 3 deacons) but his appearance that night was special. Before jumping into politics, Senator Lankford was a Christian camp director of the largest Christian youth camps in the country. It was at one of his camps that I was baptized in the swimming pool, and he had booked my Dad for over a decade to preach there. They had seen many come to Christ together over the years, and now he had snuck in to say goodbye. At the end of the service, Senator Lankford offered closing remarks and the closing prayer. Because of Waterfront Church's stance on remaining separate from politics in ultimate defense of the gospel and scripture, to this day, Senator Lankford is the only politician to speak publicly at Waterfront Church. He did so as a friend of my Dad.

That night, after the service, Senator Lankford asked Dad if they could get some time alone to talk. They went up to the room on the top floor of the Marriott where Scott and David dutifully waited outside. We had just finished cleaning up when my phone buzzed. It was Dad and he was inviting me into the room with he and the senator. I felt like Timothy walking into the upper room to meet with Paul and Peter. When I got to the room, the two were trading stories of camps and revivals they had done together over the years. I sat quietly as Dad told the senator how proud he was of him. There was a mutual admiration between the two. I don't recall ever saying a word. I felt so privileged to just be in the room. Honestly, that's how the Waterfront Church vision has made me feel as well. I just can't believe God would let me be in the room. As their conversation ended, both men got teary eyed. This would be the last time they would see each other this side of heaven. They parted the way Godly men should part for what feels like he last time—in prayer for each other to strive to finish the race. That will always go down as one of my favorite D.C. moments.

I walked the two blocks home that night thinking about what was to come the next day when truth hit me like a ton of bricks. Of all things, I was thinking about what to wear because I knew there would be pictures being taken at the Capitol the next day. All of the sudden I had realized that the day Dad would be at the Capitol was March 17, 2015.

It was St. Patrick's Day! Oh, my goodness! The old man with the white beard was Dad! The young man in the green shirt was me!

We would be together in the Capitol rotunda—tomorrow! How had this happened? How had I seen this more than a decade before? What did it mean? I was a wreck. I went into Autumn and told her—she was in disbelief. We could not possibly have engineered this moment. It had been orchestrated by God himself. Autumn and I prayed and gave glory to God that day. He is the God who keeps his promises. He is the God who holds the future. He is the God who sees me. He is the one true God. Why had he shown me this day all those years ago? Answers come in time when you brain has the capacity to handle it. The next day would be one for the books. Just before bed, I pulled my green shirt out of my closet and prayed I'd be ready.

Chapter 23:
Saint Patrick's Day

The next morning. I was up early. Just like launch day, March 16 and 17 blend together because I didn't sleep much. Autumn got a sitter for Jack and Harper, but we decided to bring Lulu, who was just about to turn 5 with us for the day. When we got to the hotel, Dad was in a brand-new suit. He never wore a suit unless it was absolutely necessary and it was, apparently, absolutely necessary. He looked sharp. We loaded the car and headed to Congressman Neugebauer's office for instructions.

The congressman was a class act and a true friend to Waterfront Church. He and his wife, Dana, rarely missed services if they were in town and many of the congressional officials now attending Waterfront Church felt comfortable trying us out because of their testimony about us. After getting our instructions, we walked Dad to his security checkpoint and then our group was dismissed to the viewing balcony. There were so many of us up there. People from our church had turned out to see Dad pray and some people had flown in all the way from Lubbock just for the moment.

I remember sitting in the balcony so proud as we waited for the session to begin. Then, out of nowhere, Congressman Mark Meadows of North Carolina burst into the balcony looking for me. He and his wife, Debbie, have been with our church since the earliest of days thanks to the Neugebauers.

"You can't watch your Dad pray from up here," he exclaimed. "Come with me." I hopped up and went after him not fully understanding what was going on. He explained that we were headed to the Speaker's Lobby right next to the House floor so that I could greet Dad as soon as he finished praying. We walked past the security checkpoint but were stopped just shy of the Speaker's Lobby. Strangely you could hear the faint but growing sound of bagpipes echoing through the halls. Congressman Meadows asked the officials what the holdup was. The guard smiled and said, "President Obama, Vice President Biden, and the Prime Minister of Ireland are on the other side of this wall."

Our government does its best to keep from blending branches of government, but it was Saint Patrick's Day! Dad would pray his last public prayer mere meters from the President. It was like Paul before Festus at the end of his ministry. And just like every part of this journey, it has been a surprise. I couldn't believe it. About that time, when it seemed like we were going to be shut out, one of our 28 charter Waterfront Church members, Jenn Jett, was walking past us through the hall. She immediately asked why I wasn't watching the prayer. We explained the situation and then Jenn single handedly swayed the Secret Service into letting us by at another entrance. We got to the Speaker's Lobby just in time. I remember how quiet it was. I stood in that historic room with Congressman Meadows and a few congressional pages— the ones who were tasked with pushing Dad's wheelchair. Those moments seemed like hours.

I spent time thanking God for what he had done. I thanked him for Waterfront Church and the vision for the new creation he had so faithfully given. I thanked him for reconciling my Dad and me. I thanked him for our story, and I prayed God would give Dad strength to finish. Suddenly, the House doors swung open and there was Dad, being helped on both sides by pages as he made his way to his wheelchair. It had taken so much out of him to stand. What happened next was also one of my favorite moments. Congressman Meadows waived off the pages and asked if he could be the one to push my Dad's wheelchair. The pages backed off. My eyes filled with tears. Congressman Meadows began telling my Dad that his legacy lives on in me. He told him how he was growing in his faith and how God had blessed his life with Waterfront Church. Congressman Meadows cried as he told him. Dad cried as he listened. And then, I'm still not sure how this happened because we never talked about it, but Congressman Meadows ended our time together— in the Capitol rotunda. He hugged us and then left.

The old man with the white beard and the young man in the green shirt, standing together in the Capitol rotunda. Dad looked at me crying and said, "You saw this." I had and I still can't believe it. He sat in his chair and I stood next to him. We just stared at each other. Minutes later we were joined by the group. They rushed in like a tidal wave. The moment had passed, but there would be time later to process. There would be years later to process. We did some light sightseeing in the area at the Library of Congress, but Dad was beyond exhausted. We took him back to the hotel, and he was too tired to even get out of his suit. That night would end up being the last sermon he ever preached, and he did it at Waterfront Church.

Our church was less than a year old, but it would be the landing strip for Dad's ministry. He preached in his suit. He never preached in a suit, but he did the last time. I don't remember much about his sermon. I remember being genuinely concerned he wouldn't finish because he could barely keep himself together. I could see Scott trying to make eye contact with me to cut Dad off, but there was no way. Scott was the ultimate protector. God would carry Dad through— he had to. God had already done so much that day. It wasn't going to end with a bullpen preacher. They took Dad to his room immediately after he preached. We were receiving people for decisions in the Marriott hallway because the room was so full. I'll never forget my Dad's eyes staring up at me.

"Can you finish the revival for me tonight?" He asked. "I know you'll do great." It was bigger than the revival. It was Elijah and Elisha. I wanted to beg him to stay but he couldn't. He was too weak. He grabbed mine and Autumn's hands and prayed for us right there in the hallway while the final songs of worship were being sung on the other side of the doors. He was giving us his blessing, and not just our family. He was blessing the church as well. And then he left. What an ending to truly unmatched day. Scripted from top to bottom by God himself.

Chapter 24:
Thank You

Originally, Dad was supposed to stay and preach on Wednesday as a conclusion to the revival, but he was so sick from the week, that he needed to go home to Lubbock early Wednesday morning. When we drove him to the airport, he was a bit out of his head. He was singing and being funny, but there was a truly erratic nature to it. Putting him on the plane was hard, but I had plans to fly into Lubbock the following week to see him. He told me over and over how proud he was of me. He joked with Jack and sang to Lulu. He even told us how beautiful baby Harper was.

Almost as soon as he got home, he went into the hospital for the last time. I headed to Lubbock as soon as I could. Dad had a rule. I could come back to visit him during the week, but I had to be back at Waterfront Church to preach on Sundays.

"You have to teach your people that when they hurt there is no better place for them to be than around other believers." He was right again. When I got to the hospital to see Dad it was very late. My sister was there, my mom was there, and of course, Scott was there. My sister and mom were headed home, so it would just be me and Scott for the overnight shift.

When they left, Dad asked if I would help keep him awake. "I'm always lesser after I sleep these days," he said. "Keep me awake." Now, Dad loved horrible pun jokes. Over the years, he had perfected the art of telling the cheesy joke. I found a website with hundreds of them, and we just started reading them until about 2 a.m. He laughed and laughed and then eventually dozed off. He couldn't stay awake forever. I was sleeping on the couch in his room and Scott was standing guard on the recliner. About 4 a.m. Dad woke up suddenly needing to go to the bathroom. He was startled and tried to stand but his legs were too weak.

Scott and I both sprung from the bed to catch him and by the grace of God, we did just before he fell. I took hold of Dad, and Scott ran out the door to get the nurse. Somehow in the process, Dad and I came forehead to forehead with my arms holding him up around his. His eyes looked straight into mine. He had gray eyes, and they were so piercing. His face was gaunt, and he was out of breath. "Thank you." He said. It was just he and I in the room at this point. "Sure thing, pops," I quipped. "No," he said without breaking gaze. "Thank you." He meant for all of it—for following him around when I was a kid, for pursuing him after the Paradigm bible study at Texas Tech, for forgiving his shortcomings, for letting him teach me how to walk with God and preach with conviction, for being his best friend and coming all the way across the country to be with him through the messy finale of his life. "I love you, pops."

He went downhill fast after that. Dad preached his last sermon at Waterfront Church on March 17, 2015 and he took his last breath on earth on April 1, 2015. I was sitting with Scott in the waiting room when he died, and my mom and sister were by his side. He finished his race. He lived nine months longer than his diagnosis, so he called those months his "extra innings." He asked me to preach his funeral, and it was one of the hardest things I'd ever done. But, if church planting had taught me anything, it was that God would carry me on the days I didn't have strength to stand if I just had faith. Four days after Dad died was Easter Sunday. It is so fitting when a pastor dies near Easter. It is the celebration of the hope we have in Jesus Christ! Waterfront Church had its largest day ever at that point. And then there were 150. The church was 8 months old and it was headed primed to not only survive but thrive.

Chapter 25:
He's Not Here

The weeks following Dad's death were hard, but God had given me plenty of other things to think about, like the completion of the vision. That heavenly ordained moment was so powerful. Why was that the moment that God chose to freeze in time? And now that it was over, what would he do next? Would there be another vision? I was open to anything, just like the day my senior year at the foot of my futon. Around that time, my mom messaged and asked if I'd come and help her clear out my Dad's office at the church. They had hired an interim pastor, and it needed to become his office. I got to the church, that I myself had worked at for years, and it was late. My flight had been a little behind and everyone was leaving the office just as I was showing up.

My mom was waiting there for me, but she had not actually been in the office since the day he went to the hospital. His drink from McDonald's was still sitting on his desk. She walked in for about 30 seconds, burst into tears, and then told me she was sorry, but that she just couldn't do this. I heard her car speed off and then I was alone in the room. I don't know why I did this, but in that moment I looked at the ceiling and tried to talk to my Dad. I know that this is poor theology, but it is just what I did. It seemed like a moment he would have appreciated. I said to the ceiling tile, "Well, Dad, here we are."

I missed talking to him so badly. I missed telling him all about the church and my kids. I missed helping him troubleshoot problems at the church in Texas, and I missed bragging back and forth about what God had been up to in our lives. I just felt so very alone. And that's when a second miracle happened. Only twice in my life have I ever heard what I believe to be the audible voice of God. The first was in the vision all those years ago, and the second was in my father's old office.

The Holy Spirit spoke saying, "He's not here, but I am, and I've always been here." The tears began to flow. He was right. Dad was not of this world anymore, and my Dad was not the Holy Spirit either.

All of the sudden, I understood why God had given the initial vision all those years ago. He was teaching me to depend on him above all else. And not just so I would plant a church in D.C. or heal the bond with my father. God wanted me to know Him and trust Him more. He wanted to be my source of strength and wisdom. He wanted to show me the extent of his love. He wanted to show me that if I would seek first his kingdom and his righteousness, that all these other things would be added to me. The deepest desires of my heart would be added to me. To live a life of meaning, to marry my soulmate and ministry partner, to preach the gospel and start a church, to live a life of meaning for the kingdom, and to have my father's friendship and respect. I got everything I ever dreamed of when I surrendered to Jesus. "If anyone is in Christ, they are a new creation. The old is gone, and behold, the new has come."

The new creation God had been working on all this time was my relationship with him. Waterfront Church is a miracle, but my relationship with God is my reason for getting out of bed in the morning. I love my wife and kids more than anything on the planet, but I love them best when I love God just a bit more. My father's respect and friendship are things I greatly cherish, but my confidence is found in Christ alone. The world and its treasures will all pass away but in Christ, we gain everything, for eternity and today.

And then there were 2 of us. God and me.